965
3-ne

OPERA

*A scene from Mussorgsky's Boris Godunov, with
Ezio Pinza in the title role.*

OPERA

CHARLES HAMM

Professor of Music
University of Illinois

Allyn and Bacon, Inc.
Boston, 1966

*To my father
and the memory
of my mother*

PREFACE

※ ※ ※

This is a book about opera, not operas.

A tradition has been built up in this country that opera is the most difficult, intellectual, esoteric of all art forms, one which can be enjoyed or appreciated only after a rigorous period of apprenticeship. Whether carried out with the aid of books, lectures, college courses, radio programs, or individual instruction, this apprenticeship usually takes the form of a study of operas—in the plural. The way one learns to "enjoy" *Madame Butterfly*, for instance, is to study it enough to learn who the major characters are and what their relationships are to one another, what they say in certain key scenes, and what some of the music sounds like. If such a program is carried out faithfully enough, the budding "opera lover" may reach the point of being able to attend a performance and have the proper muscular responses: applaud when he should applaud; cry a bit at the end; and leave the opera house humming one or more of the most familiar tunes. But even though what he has learned enables him to respond to this particular opera in these several superficial ways, it is of little use in coming to terms with another one. In order to "enjoy" a performance of *Faust* or *Carmen*, he must do the same homework for these operas, and the number of works he can learn to enjoy is limited by the time and energy he has for this sort of business.

A German or Italian or Russian, by contrast, goes to the opera house with the expectation that the opera he is to see that evening will make itself understandable to *him*. The homework has been done by the librettist, composer, director, producer, and singers—not by the audience. It is assumed that a show will be offered which will be attractive and comprehensible, musically and dramatically, to anyone of normal intelligence who has some interest in theater and music, and if this does not happen it does not occur to the audience to blame itself. It seems no coincidence that opera enjoys a popularity in these countries unmatched in America.

This book is addressed to those persons, with or without training in music, who are interested in penetrating the *mystique* and snobbishness which too often surrounds opera in this country, who would like to be able to attend an operatic performance and respond to what they see and hear in an intelligent and critical fashion. It sets out to explain the structure and mechanics of opera in as simple a way as possible, and to give some insight into the workings of the composer and his relationship to his librettist. The component parts of an opera are discussed and illustrated separately, and a complete act of a successful work is examined in detail as a demonstration of the integration of these various elements in an effective musical-dramatic work.

This book will be most effective if sections from the various operas discussed are listened to immediately. For this reason, I have selected my examples mostly from those operas popular today and most readily accessible on recordings.

When quoting from a libretto, I have used translations as nearly contemporary with the opera as possible. Some of these make curious reading today, but I believe that they more nearly capture the spirit of the original than do more recent translations. Those not otherwise identified are my own.

Though I am a historian by belief and profession, I have not written a history of opera, since I am not convinced that a strictly historical approach is the most effective one in leading the nonprofessional to maximum enjoyment and understanding of those works he is likely to encounter in stage performance. Nor have I dealt with aesthetics, except in incidental fashion; here again I feel that this is an area most effectively dealt with after a person has some grasp of the basic structures, techniques, and nature of opera. I have often had the melancholy experience, in my teaching of advanced courses in opera, of discovering that students had somehow never learned many of the most elementary things about the form; it is the modest aim of this book to furnish a foundation for the enjoyment of opera, or for more advanced study of it. For anyone interested in going beyond this book to a study of the history and aesthetics of opera, I recommend two excellent books in English, Donald Grout's *A Short History of Opera* and Joseph Kerman's *Opera as Drama*.

This book was conceived and partly written while I was a member of the faculty of Newcomb College of Tulane University in New Orleans. I gratefully acknowledge a summer grant from the Tulane University Council on Research which facilitated my work. I am also indebted to Richard Jackson and Ellsworth Snyder, colleagues of mine at the time, who were always ready to talk about opera; many of my ideas were formed or clarified in conversations with them. Adam Carse's excellent *The Orchestra from Beethoven to Berlioz* was a useful source for Chapter VII.

Jeffrey Kurtzman and Wallace Rave helped with the thankless task of copying musical examples. I am particularly indebted to Susan Dwight, of the staff of Allyn & Bacon, for her intelligent and careful work on the manuscript and for a host of valuable suggestions.

Charles Hamm

Urbana, Illinois

CONTENTS

OPERA

THE SINGERS

It would be impossible to begin a discussion of opera anywhere but with the singers. Opera without an orchestra can still be opera—hundreds of performances take place in this country to the accompaniment of a single piano. Opera without costumes and without sets can still be opera, of sorts. But opera without singers is impossible. Its great moments come when fine artists sing beautifully in dramatic situations. The same scene played in an orchestral transcription cannot possibly have the same effect.

It is true that too much of the writing on opera deals with them, and that at certain times in the history of opera more attention has been paid to them as individuals than to the form itself. Many of them have deliberately built up their own personalities to the point at which they cannot be subordinated to the drama supposedly unfolding on the stage, and in an attempt to call attention to themselves and their voices have wilfully ignored composers' stage directions, dynamic markings, and even pitches. Singers squabble among themselves, with producers and directors, and even with composers. Jealousies among them may make the casting of an opera difficult and performances unpredictable. Still, opera revolves around them; opera without singers is no longer what opera is all about.

THE SINGER AS AN INDIVIDUAL

No two opera singers are alike in personality or appearance —nor are they alike in voice. Each voice has its own timbre, its own range, its own good features, its own limitations. A true connoisseur of operatic singing can identify any singer by his voice just as easily as by his photograph.

Ideally each role in an opera would be written for a specific singer. The composer, knowing which singer would take each part, could write so as to take advantage of the best things the singer could do and could carefully avoid passages which might reveal defects. A certain soprano, for example, might have good high notes and a strong lower register but a dull spot for a few notes in the middle range. The composer, knowing this, could easily design his music so that she would not be called on to sing these weak notes at important spots. A tenor might have trouble with the *e* vowel; the composer could work with the librettist to avoid this sound in key situations. There might be a contralto with exceptional low notes but an unusually thin upper register, a soprano with a good trill, a baritone whose voice tended to wobble more the lower it went, a bass with an exceptionally agile and flexible voice, a tenor with a good high D, a coloratura who found it impossible to sing her lowest notes without going sharp. The composer, knowing all this, could exploit the strengths of the voices in his cast and also avoid troublesome spots.

Throughout the history of opera composers have written roles for specific singers. Gluck wrote the part of Orpheus in his *Orfeo ed Euridice* for the male contralto Gaetano Guadagni. The vocal limitations of the part of Papageno in Mozart's *The Magic Flute* are explainable by the fact that the librettist, Schikaneder, who was more proficient as a comic actor than as a singer, created this role. Handel wrote parts in his London operas specifically for the contralto Senesino, the bass Boschi, and the soprano Anastasia Robinson. The part of Rosina in Rossini's *The Barber of Seville* cannot be sung by any of our modern singers as it was first written. Rossini planned it for the special talents of the great contralto Isabella Colbran, but contraltos since have lacked the agility for the part, and it has been rewritten for coloratura soprano. Bellini's *I Puritani* is seldom done today, one reason being that the principal tenor part was written for Rubini, who had an enormous range and the ability to sustain a high tessitura (mean range) longer than most later tenors. In this century, Benjamin Britten has written a succession of tenor roles for the peculiar talents of the English tenor Peter Pears (the title roles in *Peter Grimes* and *Albert Herring,* Quint in *The Turn of the Screw*), Menotti planned the role of the Mother in *The Consul* for Marie

Powers, and Kurt Weill wrote the part of Jenny in *Die Dreigro-schenoper* for Lotte Lenya.

But these are exceptions. Most composers, even when they know that their work will be performed first by a certain company, are hopeful that it will be performed later by others. Most operatic roles are conceived by the composer for a type of voice, rather than for an individual singer. Even when he knows that a certain singer will take the part in its first performance, he will not let the peculiarities and limitations of this voice shape the music he writes so that it is too difficult or too simple for other singers.

Even though no two voices are alike, there are conventional groupings by range and quality. Any two tenor voices will have points of difference, but there will be more similarities between them than between one of them and a bass voice. Differences among four tenor voices can be detected, but two of them may sound more similar to one another than to either of the other two. As individual as voices are, they still can be roughly grouped. A composer can write a part in an opera for a certain type of voice rather than for an individual singer, designate the type of voice that he has in mind for this part, and know that wherever the opera is performed the role will be sung by someone with a voice corresponding more or less closely to what he has in mind.

CLASSIFICATION OF VOICES

The most basic grouping of voices is by sex, into male and female voices. In singing, as in speaking, most female voices are higher in pitch than most male voices.

A slightly more refined but still elementary division is into high and low female voices and high and low male voices. Much of the choral music sung by church, school, and community groups is written or arranged for four groups of voices: high female (soprano), low female (alto), high male (tenor), and low male (bass). The approximate range of each of these voices is:

For choral music written in more than four parts, necessitating further division of the voices, the sopranos are simply split into two groups designated as first sopranos and second sopranos, and the altos, tenors, and basses are similarly divided.

Such a division and classification of voices, on the basis of range alone, works well enough for choral music. In group singing the desired effect is for each voice to sacrifice its individual sound to the over-all effect.

Not so in opera, in which the ideal from the beginning has been the glorification of the individual voice. Composers have recognized and written for a much wider variety of voices, differing from one another not only in range but also in quality. For example, Virgil Thomson calls for the following voices in his opera *The Mother of Us All* (with a libretto by Gertrude Stein).

light lyric soprano	Angel More
lyric soprano	Lillian Russell
soprano	Gertrude S., Henrietta M.
dramatic soprano	Susan B. Anthony
high mezzo-soprano	Constance Fletcher
mezzo-soprano	Isabel Wentworth, Jenny Reefer
contralto	Anne, Indiana Elliot, Anna Hope
romantic tenor	John Adams
tenor	Andrew Johnson, Thaddeus Stevens, Jo
high baritone	Herman Atlan
baritone	Virgil T., Chris the Citizen, Gloster Heming, Donald Gallup
bass baritone	Henry B., Ulysses S. Grant, Indiana Elliot's Brother
bass	Daniel Webster, Anthony Comstock

Thomson differentiates among seven different types of female voices (including six types of sopranos) and six types of male voices.

Few composers have gone this far in classifying voices. Actually, until recent decades, most seem to have gone no further in differentiating among voice types than have composers of choral music. For several centuries voices were designated not by the terms *soprano*, *tenor*, and the like, but by different clefs. Today both sopranos and altos sing from parts written in the treble clef, basses sing from the bass clef, and tenor parts are written in either the treble or bass clef. But until the end of the nineteenth century soprano parts were written in the soprano clef, alto parts in the alto clef, tenor parts in the tenor clef, and bass parts in the bass clef—and there was no further designation of voice types or differentiation within these classifications. Thus Mozart's *The Magic Flute*, using only three clefs, seems to suggest that Mozart thought of only three voice classifications.

soprano	Three Ladies
	Queen of the Night
	Pamina
	Papagena
tenor	Tamino
	Monostatos
	First Priest
bass	Papageno
	Sarastro
	Second Priest

And when, in the nineteenth century, composers began designating voice types by classifications rather than by multiple clefs, they still differentiated among no more than the three or four basic voices. Cherubini and Meyerbeer call for only sopranos, tenors, and basses in their operas, and so late and progressive a work as Wagner's *Die Meistersinger* calls for no more than these same three voices in its large cast.

But these "ancient" composers knew as much as or more than composers of today about different types of voices. Despite the fact that their scores do not openly advertise it, they wrote for just as great a variety of voices. An examination of range, tessitura, use of orchestra, and text makes it clear that Mozart was writing for many more different types of voices than is suggested by the three clefs. The roles in *The Magic Flute* would be cast today as:

Three Ladies	soprano
	mezzo-soprano
	contralto
Queen of the Night	coloratura soprano
Pamina	lyric soprano
Papagena	high lyric soprano

Tamino	lyric tenor
Monostatos	low tenor
First Priest	tenor
Papageno	light baritone
Sarastro	bass
Second Priest	baritone

And even though Wagner groups Hans Sachs, Beckmesser, and Pogner together as basses in *Die Meistersinger,* they must be cast with three rather different types of voices. Likewise the parts of Walter von Stolzing and David must be sung by quite different kinds of tenors.

One of the necessary skills for a composer of opera is and always has been a knowledge of a wide range of different types of voices and the ability to write music which shows off each type to best advantage.

Female Voices. The term *soprano* is a general designation for high-pitched female voices. Within this group, the highest voices of all are known today as coloratura sopranos. The distinguishing features of this voice are its range, which may extend as much as an octave above other sopranos; its clear, light, sometimes thin, bell-

like quality; and its agility. Most coloratura soprano roles feature rapid scale passages, arpeggios, repeated notes, trills, and other technical passages. The term *coloratura* itself refers to virtuoso singing, not to the range of the voice. Formerly coloratura singing was not confined to high sopranos; there were coloratura contraltos, tenors, and even basses. But the art of singing has progressed in the last century in a direction which has de-emphasized agility in all voices but the coloratura soprano. Among the currently popular roles for this voice are The Queen of the Night in Mozart's *The Magic Flute,* Lucia in Donizetti's *Lucia di Lammermoor,* and Zerbinetta in Richard Strauss's *Ariadne auf Naxos.*

The most basic division among the rest of the sopranos is into dramatic and lyric. The distinction is not in the range, which is the same for the two voices, but in the quality of the voice. A lyric soprano's voice is usually fairly light, warm, and flexible, while the dramatic soprano has a heavier, darker, and larger sound, forceful enough to carry over the heavy orchestration which often accompanies a dramatic role. Descriptions of the difference in sound between these two voices are of course an unsatisfactory substitute for hearing them in performance or on recordings. Familiar lyric soprano roles are Mimi in Puccini's *La Bohème*, Susannah in Mozart's *The Marriage of Figaro*, and Sophia in Strauss's *Der Rosenkavalier;* dramatic roles are Donna Anna in Mozart's *Don Giovanni*, Leonora in Beethoven's *Fidelio*, Isolde in Wagner's *Tristan und Isolde*, and Santuzza in Mascagni's *Cavalleria Rusticana*.

The dividing line between lyric and dramatic soprano is by no means always clear. Some voices have some dramatic qualities and some lyric qualities, some voices are flexible enough for both lyric and dramatic roles. Likewise with the roles themselves: some contain passages most effectively performed by a lyric and other passages seemingly requiring a dramatic, some are regularly sung by both types of soprano.

The term *spinto* is sometimes used to describe a voice lying between lyric and dramatic, a voice with both qualities. Soprano roles which demand such a voice are called spinto roles. Among them are Leonora in Verdi's *Il Trovatore*, Leonora in the same composer's *La Forza del Destino*, and Agatha in Carl Maria von Weber's *Der Freischütz*.

Lying between the highest and the lowest female voices is the mezzo-soprano, or simply mezzo. Though it may be called upon for an occasional quite high note, the tessitura of this voice is somewhat lower than that of the true soprano.

In sound, the voice is heavier, darker, and somewhat less flexible than higher soprano voices, often approaching the true contralto. Among mezzo roles are Marina in Mussorgsky's *Boris Godunov* and Suzuki in Puccini's *Madame Butterfly*.

The rarest of all female voices is the genuine contralto. Many composers never wrote for this voice, and many of those who did write contralto parts in their operas made such roles minor ones, because of the difficulty in finding first-rate voices of this type. The range overlaps more than an octave of the tenor range, so that contraltos often sing lower than tenors.

The sound is dark, heavy, rich, vibrant. A contralto singing in her lowest register sounds nothing at all like a tenor singing in the same range—the tenor sound, in the upper register, has a brilliance which contrasts sharply with the sound of a contralto. The contralto voice, in contrast, has a tendency to sound covered or even muffled, and it is difficult for even the best singers to project sufficiently if the composer has backed their part with heavy orchestration.

True contralto roles are La Cieca in Ponchielli's *La Gioconda,* Lucia in *Cavalleria Rusticana,* and Madame Flora in Menotti's *The Medium.* Since so few major roles have been written for this voice, contraltos are forced to look for roles elsewhere. Amneris in Verdi's *Aida,* Azucena in his *Il Trovatore,* Delilah in Saint-Saens' *Samson et Delilah,* and Ulrica in Verdi's *A Masked Ball* are commonly sung by contraltos, but each was thought of by its composer as a mezzo-soprano role. Contraltos have even gone as far afield as the soprano repertoire, doing such parts as Carmen. Here again there is no sharp dividing line between two different voices, in this case mezzo and contralto. Quite possibly a voice which Verdi would have considered a mezzo would be labeled a contralto today.

Male Voices. In earlier centuries there was some cultivation of the *falsettist,* a male voice which ascended into the soprano range by way of falsetto, but opera composers of the last two hundred years have not made use of male voices that ascend into the extreme upper register. Such voices have been regarded as freaks and ignored by composers and voice teachers. The highest male voice recognized in opera is the tenor, in range an octave below the soprano.

Like sopranos, tenors are classified as lyric or dramatic, the difference being not of range but of quality of voice. Some tenor roles make sense only when sung by a light, clear, flexible voice—Papageno in Mozart's *The Magic Flute,* Count Almaviva in Rossini's *Barber of Seville,* Des Grieux in Puccini's *Manon Lescaut*—while others require a more forceful, robust voice capable of more volume and more endurance—Otello in Verdi's operatic version of the play, Wagner's Siegfried, Canio in Leoncavallo's *I Pagliacci.* Some tenors sing both lyric and dramatic roles. Some roles do not fall clearly on one side or the other of the dividing line, and some people classify such roles as Radames in Verdi's *Aida* and Cavaradossi in Puccini's *La Tosca* as spinto tenor roles.

A special variety of dramatic tenor is needed for certain German operas; often called a *Heldentenor* (*Held* is German for *hero*), such a singer needs uncommon endurance and the ability to sustain a high tessitura for prolonged scenes.

Among all singers, but particularly tenors, there is a strong secondary classification by nationality which sometimes takes precedence over classification into dramatic or lyric. Italian-born and -trained tenors almost never sing the German repertoire, and German tenors often avoid Italian opera. Some Italian tenors have large voices and some small, but their characteristic open-throated, legato type of singing works beautifully for Italian opera. Germans tend to articulate consonants more forcefully and to sing with a somewhat coarser tone, which is just the way Beethoven and Wagner and Strauss should be sung. It is mostly the singers of other nationalities—the Americans and Spaniards and Swedes and Australians and English—who type themselves as either lyric or dramatic.

A singer with a voice slightly lower in range than a true tenor and with a somewhat heavier and richer sound is classified as a baritone. This voice has the same relationship to the tenor as a mezzo has to a soprano. Its range is,

although it is at its best in the middle and upper parts of this range, and composers tend to avoid the bottom third of the register. Some baritones think of themselves as being either lyric or dramatic, and it is true that some roles are better sung by a lighter, warmer, more legato voice (the older Germont in Verdi's *La Traviata,* Wolfram in

Wagner's *Tannhäuser*); and others benefit from a more forceful, larger sound (Scarpia in Puccini's *La Tosca*, Gunther in Wagner's *Götterdämmerung*, Macbeth in Verdi's *Macbeth*). Sometimes a singer specializing in German opera will call himself a Helden-baritone. Other baritones with light, high voices of a particular quality (slightly nasal) classify themselves as "French" baritones.

Singers who find the baritone range comfortable but who have heavier voices than most baritones and can also sing forcefully in the bottom part of the range are called bass-baritones. Few roles call specifically for this voice; such singers do dramatic baritone parts and also the higher bass roles. They are handy to have around.

Unlike the contralto, the lowest male voice, the bass, has been found in abundance throughout the history of opera and the repertoire is liberally sprinkled with good bass roles. The range is:

The bass voice is usually rich, dark, heavy, powerful, and not at all agile. Some basses manage to be lyric, some more dramatic. Popular bass roles are Sarastro in *The Magic Flute*, Pimen in *Boris Godunov*, and Mephistopheles in Boito's most successful opera.

Like their female counterparts, the contraltos, basses often stray up into roles actually written for other voices. Mussorgsky specified that the role of Boris Godunov was to be sung by a baritone, but it is now traditionally done by a bass. Basses may raid baritone territory for such choice parts as Escamillo in *Carmen*.

The term *basso profundo* is sometimes used to describe a singer with an unusually deep bass voice. Another term sometimes encountered is *basso buffo*. Some secondary bass parts are comic, and certain singers have made a career of specializing in such roles. They usually do not have impressive vocal equipment, and some of them have been so limited vocally that their delivery often bordered on speech rather than singing; many have not been true basses at all and have done baritone as well as bass parts. Among the roles done by such singers are Leporello in Mozart's *Don Giovanni*, Varlaam in *Boris Godunov*, and Beckmesser in Wagner's *Die Meistersinger*.

Such singers belong to a much larger group usually referred to as *comprimario* singers. These are singers of all voices who lack the vocal equipment to do major roles and who make a career of smaller parts, often character or comic, making up for their vocal deficiencies by their stage manner, musicianship, and character portrayal. Such singers are by no means necessarily inferior to singers who take the star roles—their talents are simply different. Often the success of a production depends just as much on the *comprimario* singers as on those who take the major roles, and many a *comprimario* is as much an artist in his own right as any of the more famous singers.

❦ VOICES AND ROLES

Composers of the last several centuries have followed certain conventions when deciding what voice type to assign to each of the characters in an opera. The most obvious of these conventions is that lower voices are normally used for older characters, higher voices for younger. Thus basses frequently portray old men (Pimen in *Boris Godunov*, Arkel in *Pelléas et Mélisande*), baritones often find themselves cast as middle-aged (Giorgio Germont in *La Traviata*, Lord Ashton in *Lucia di Lammermoor*, Rigoletto), and tenors are most often called upon to sing the parts of young men (Rodolfo in *La Bohème*, Romeo in Gounod's *Romeo et Juliet*). This is purely a convention; there is no basis for it in nature. A boy's voice is treble until it changes in his early teens, but once this change takes place there is no further deepening of his speaking voice. If anything, there is a tendency for it to become higher in pitch as he matures, and the voices of quite old men may become shriller, not deeper. But it is a useful convention in opera, one which audiences have accepted readily.

Casting of female characters follows the same convention. Contraltos often portray older women (La Cieca, the mother in *La Gioconda*, the old Baroness in Barber's *Vanessa*), many mezzos spend much of their time singing and acting the parts of ladies who have lost the bloom of youth (Herodias in Strauss's *Salome*, Ortrud in Wagner's *Lohengrin*), and sopranos, particularly lyric sopranos, must be ready to assume the part of a young woman (Susanna in *The Marriage of Figaro*, Cho-Cho-San in *Madame Butterfly*, Monica in Menotti's *The Medium*).

Many operas contain family groups among the characters, and such groups are almost invariably arranged with parents cast as lower voices than their children. In *Pelléas et Mélisande*, Arkel, the grandfather, is a bass, the older brother Golaud is a baritone, and the younger brother Pelléas is a tenor. In Strauss's *Elektra*, Clytemnestra, the mother, is a mezzo, and her daughters Elektra and Chrysothemis are sopranos. Prince Igor is a baritone in Borodin's opera, and his son Vladimir is a tenor. In Puccini's *Turandot*, Timur is a bass and Calaf, his son, is a tenor. Marguerite is a soprano in Boito's *Mefistofele*, her mother is a contralto; there is similar casting in Charpentier's *Louise*, in *La Gioconda*, and in Meyerbeer's *La Prophète*.

Massenet, in his operatic version of *Werther*, indicates the age of some of the characters in his cast list. Here too there is exact correspondence between age and type of voice.

Werther, 23	tenor
Albert, 25	baritone
Le Bailli, 50	baritone or bass
Sophie, 15	soprano
Charlotte, 20	mezzo-soprano

The casts of many operas call for children. Although it is possible to find children who can sing, until quite recently composers felt that a child's voice with its peculiar quality had no place in opera. The usual solution was to have children's parts sung by female voices. Thus the part of Yniold, the young son of Golaud in *Pelléas et Mélisande*, is sung by a soprano, as is Tell's son Jemmy in Rossini's *Guillaume Tell*. The greatest problem with such casting is a visual one, finding a woman small enough and skilled enough in stage movement to create the illusion that she is a child. Some composers have made a distinction in their casting between female and male children, using sopranos for the former and mezzos for the latter. Hansel is a mezzo in Humperdinck's *Hansel und Gretel*, his sister is a soprano; the shepherd boy in *Tosca* is a mezzo, as is Boris's son Theodore in *Boris Godunov*. This is again a convention. Children's speaking voices are treble; some are higher or lower than others, but this variation is an individual matter having nothing to do with the sex of the child.

Cherubino in Mozart's *The Marriage of Figaro* is an adolescent, a boy in his teens. The composer wanted to emphasize his boyish character by having his role sung by a higher voice than that of any of the other men in the cast. Since several roles are sung by the highest male voice, the tenor, the only way Mozart could differentiate Cherubino vocally was by writing his part for a female voice. Cherubino is a soprano, even though we would judge by his nervous interest in the opposite sex that his speaking voice should have changed to tenor or bass. The illusion works, given a soprano who can carry off the ticklish business of dressing and moving like a young boy.

The practice of having the parts of young boys sung by sopranos or mezzos is merely an extension of the convention of having the roles of children sung by adult females. The difficulty which present-day American audiences have in accepting this convention increases with the age and maturity of the child in question. Strauss has cast Octavian as a mezzo in *Der Rosenkavalier*, but he is hardly a boy; he is the Marschallin's lover, and the two are discovered in bed together when the first-act curtain opens. Their opening love duet, for soprano and mezzo, must be heard as a duet between a man and a woman, and later scenes between Octavian and Sophia, a lyric soprano, must also be heard as male-female scenes.

A second convention which guides the composer in his casting is that certain types of voices are commonly associated with certain personality and character traits. Many people automatically and unconsciously relate a deep, resonant speaking voice to an imposing, strong, masculine personality and a high-pitched voice to a weaker, more ineffectual character. There is no more basis for this than for the convention of relating voice pitch to age, but it has been carried over to the operatic stage.

Operatic basses would be overbearing were they to identify themselves with the characters they portray on stage. Bass roles include a long list of forceful, dignified, masculine, noble, thoroughly admirable characters: Seneca in Monteverdi's *L'Incoronazione di Poppea*, Jupiter in Lully's *Isis*, King Mark in *Tristan und Isolde*, the King in *Aida*, King Henry of Germany in *Lohengrin*, Calkas the high priest in Walton's *Troilus and Cressida*, among many other men of nobility and authority. The medium-range male voices, dramatic tenor and baritone, are most often used for heroic and virile characters: Escamillo in *Carmen*, the title role in Giordano's *Andrea Chenier*, Siegfried, Boris Godunov. Lighter tenors at the best assume roles of young lovers (Count Almaviva in Rossini's *The Barber of Seville*, Werther in Massenet's *Werther*, Rodolfo in *La Bohème*), and otherwise find a variety of weak, ineffectual roles to be their lot (Don Ottavio in Mozart's *Don Giovanni*, Little Bat in Carlisle Floyd's *Susanna*, the Fool in *Boris Godunov*).

There is even a sharp difference between low-voiced villians and high-voiced ones. The basses and baritones are a thoroughly scandalous lot, but they at least have strongly defined personalities. Such characters as Pizarro in *Fidelio*, Sparafucile in *Rigoletto*, Hagen in Wagner's *Götterdämmerung*, and Scarpia in *Tosca* are so enthusiastically devoted to the propagation of evil that they earn a sort of grudging respect. The villainous tenors, on the other hand, are a sorry group: the ridiculous Monostatos in *The Magic Flute*, whose attempted evil deeds are frustrated and turned into comedy; Sporting Life, the

*The Canadian bass, George London, in the first act of
Wagner's The Flying Dutchman. Bayreuth, 1959.*

treacherous dope-peddler in Gershwin's *Porgy and Bess;* the sadistic captain in Berg's *Wozzeck,* whose warped mind helps bring on the final tragedy.

In many operas, contrasts in type of voice are used by the composer to play up contrasts in character. The "hero" of Stravinsky's *The Rake's Progress,* Tom Rakewell, is a shallow, vain, opportunistic person who is shadowed throughout by Nick, a symbol of evil, but a much more positive character than Tom. Tom is a tenor, Nick a bass-baritone. Mozart's Don Giovanni is an aggressive, resourceful, thoroughly masculine character (a baritone) who is contrasted favorably with the well-meaning but ineffectual Don Ottavio (a tenor). Don Giovanni is finally done in—not by the likes of a tenor, but by the Commandante, a bass.

Composers have done less matching of type of voice to personality with female characters than with male, probably because fewer associations exist in relationship to women's speaking voices. Curiously, while a high-pitched male voice is often thought to suggest a lack of certain masculine traits, the reverse of this is not true. A low-pitched woman's voice, on the contrary, is currently considered "sexy."

An actress portraying the role of a confused, fluttery, flighty woman—of any age—is likely to fall back on a higher-pitched speaking voice than she would normally use. This association is sometimes made use of in opera. Many of the coloratura soprano roles of the nineteenth century are of women who for one reason or another teeter on the dividing line between sanity and madness; their "mad scenes" furnish apparent excuses for excesses of coloratura display. More recent operas, such as Menotti's *The Telephone,* use high coloratura passages to suggest a flighty or giddy personality. At the other end of the scale, composers have preferred the lower-pitched and darker-hued female voices for characters who are in some way sinister, mysterious, or even villainous. Madame Flora, the unscrupulous medium who preys on other people's misery and need in Menotti's *The Medium,* is a contralto. The scheming and treacherous Ortrud in *Lohengrin* is a mezzo. Azucena in *Il Trovatore* is not an evil person, but in the eerie scene in the gypsy camp in which she huddles over a campfire and sings of the bloody past and her desire for revenge, the low pitch and dark color of a mezzo or contralto voice gives the sinister effect needed.

Now and then a composer will cast a king as a tenor or an old woman as a soprano, but these are exceptions. The conventions of relating type of voice to age and personality are deep-rooted and are violated only for deliberate effect, or when the composer knows in advance that he will not have one or more of the voice types available.

For purposes of illustration, let us assume that it was decided to convert Tennessee Williams' *A Streetcar Named Desire*[1] into an opera and see how the composer would assign voice types to the various characters in the drama.

STANLEY KOWALSKI: "He is of medium height, about five feet eight or nine, and strongly, compactly built. Animal joy in his being is implicit in all his movements and attitudes. Since earliest manhood the center of his life has been pleasure with women. . . . Branching out from this complete and satisfying center are all the auxiliary channels of his life, such as his heartiness with men, his appreciation of rough humor, his love of good drink and food and games. . . ." He is twenty-eight or thirty years old. Certainly this role, with its overwhelming masculinity, would be assigned to one of the lower voices. Stanley would be a baritone or a bass-baritone.

HAROLD MITCHELL (MITCH): He plays poker with Stanley and his friends and in some ways is "one of the boys"—but he is different. He has a "sort of sensitive look," is worried about his sick mother, and is somewhat ineffectual in his courting of Blanche. Mitch would be cast as a tenor, partly as a contrast with the much stronger personality of Stanley, partly because of his own gentler nature, partly because he is involved in the only suggestion of romantic love in the drama.

STELLA: Stanley's wife is described by the playwright as "a gentle young woman, about twenty-five, and of a background obviously quite different from her husband's." Because of her youth and her quiet, sweet personality, she would be some sort of soprano.

BLANCHE: "She is about five years older than Stella. Her delicate beauty must avoid a strong light. There is something about her uncertain manner, as well as her white clothes, that suggests a moth." Personality would overrule age in casting this part. Making Blanche a mezzo or contralto because she is older than her sister would set up a conflict between her voice and her personality. The impression of fragility, instability, nervousness, even imminent hysteria would best be suggested by a high, light voice. Blanche should be a light lyric soprano, perhaps even a lyric-coloratura; the composer might be tempted to provide her with a few discreet coloratura flights in her giddy scenes.

[1] Copyright 1947 by Tennessee Williams.

EUNICE HUBBELL: The upstairs neighbor, a hearty, earthy type. One of the minor roles, it would probably be cast as a contralto to contrast with Stella and Blanche.

STEVE HUBBELL, PABLO GONZALES: The other members of the poker game, both small roles. No sharp personality comes through for either in the play. They would both most likely be cast for lower voices, perhaps one a baritone and the other a bass, so that Mitch would be the only tenor among the four poker players.

A YOUNG COLLECTOR: The newspaper boy who comes to collect while Blanche is in the apartment alone must be in his teens. Composers of the last century would have written this part for a female voice, maybe a mezzo, to emphasize his youth. A present-day American composer would hesitate to have a male part sung by a female, for fear that his audience would have difficulty accepting such a convention, and would set the part for a high, light tenor.

NURSE: "Divested of all the softer properties of womanhood. The Matron is a peculiarly sinister figure in her severe dress." This part would undoubtedly be sung by a contralto.

DOCTOR: "The gravity of (his) profession is exaggerated. His voice is reassuring. He supports her with his arm and leads her through the portieres." He is a strong character, a person of authority who takes over Blanche's life at the end of the drama. A bass.

OTHER VOICES

Children.   Church music has relied on children's voices for many centuries, but, as mentioned earlier, until quite recently they were not used in opera. There were sound reasons for this. Almost from the beginnings of opera a distinction was recognized between "operatic" voices and "nonoperatic" ones. Since operatic singing is largely solo work, and operas are usually done in large halls or auditoriums, one of the basic requirements of an operatic voice is that it must project enough to reach every part of the auditorium. Treble boys' voices, boy sopranos and altos, are often quite penetrating, and a group of them can easily hold their own against tenors and basses in choral music—but the sound of a single one of these voices in a large hall is quite thin and empty.

In addition, boys' treble voices have a peculiar pure, colorless, "white" sound which is appropriate for church music but is singularly inappropriate for the expression of the more earthy passions with which opera has always concerned itself. Moreover, in past centuries the opera house was often a center for many of the minor vices and crimes—gambling, prostitution, political and social intrigue—and there was a feeling that it was not the place for a child to be, for any reason.

In the present century, however, a desire for realism and a gradual breakdown in some of the time-honored conventions of opera have led to the use of children in opera.

The title role in Menotti's Christmas opera *Amahl and the Night Visitors* is the child's part most familiar to most Americans. Amahl is a crippled twelve-year-old boy; the composer specifies that the part is to be sung by a boy soprano, since the pure, colorless sound of such a voice is exactly what he wants to intensify the young, innocent, winsome nature of the character. A female soprano might stay on pitch better and make more conventional operatic sounds, but this is not what the composer is after.

Benjamin Britten has made more use of boy sopranos than any other composer; his operas are rarely without at least one. Harry in his popular comic opera *Albert Herring* is a "treble" (boy soprano); as are Miles in *The Turn of the Screw*; Sam, Gay, Jonny, and Hugh in *The Little Sweep*; Sem, Ham, and Jaffett in *Noye's Fludde*; and some of the fairies in *Midsummer Night's Dream*. Britten has also written parts for young girls. The roles of Emmy and Cis in *Albert Herring* and Flora in *The Turn of the Screw* are to be sung by girls, not women. Here again Britten wants the thin, shrill, colorless sound of an undeveloped voice, for dramatic reasons.

In the last decade other composers have written parts, some of them major roles, for children's voices. If the trend continues and the opera public becomes accustomed to it, it is probably merely a matter of time before children will be singing those children's parts in older operas which have always been sung by women. We may yet see Yniold sung by a boy soprano, or Gretel by a young girl.

Countertenor.   For many centuries the alto part in choral music was sung by men, not women; the term is derived from the Latin *altus* (high), and was used to describe the highest male voice. A good male alto has a bright, clear, sweet sound which is not large, but projects well. The voice was almost completely neglected in the nineteenth century, even in choral music, and a man with a voice naturally higher than the usual tenor had no place in the musical life of the time.

It remained for the twentieth century, with its ever-increasing passion for ancient music, to rediscover the male alto, or counter-tenor. Musicologists first supplied the information that male altos were needed for authentic performances of old music. Then, just as lutes, harpsichords, recorders, viols, and other such once-obsolete instruments enjoyed a renaissance, countertenor voices began turning up. They are much in demand now, to sing solo literature from the Renaissance and Baroque periods, to sing the alto parts in Renaissance polyphony, and even to sing solo parts in Handel oratorios.

Just as certain of our contemporary composers have been moved to write new music for ancient instruments, so a few have begun writing for the countertenor, recognizing it as a voice with a unique quality. The part of Oberon, King of the Fairies, in Britten's *Midsummer Night's Dream* is written for countertenor. The fairies over whom he rules (Cobweb, Peaseblossom, Mustardseed, Moth) are trebles (children); the effect is a sharp differentiation in sound between the fairies (countertenor, treble) and the "real" people in the play, who are the usual sopranos, altos, tenors, and basses.

It is not difficult to predict that more composers will write operatic roles for the countertenor voice in the near future. It will be interesting to see how they will treat this unusual voice, how they will handle the situation of a male singer with a range normally associated with a female. Possibly countertenors will take over roles of very young men, roles of the sort assigned to mezzos in operas of previous centuries.

The Castrati.   The part of Nero in Monteverdi's *L'Incoronazione di Poppea* is written for a soprano; the title role in Handel's *Rinaldo* was sung by an alto; Romeo in Zingarelli's *Giulietta e Romeo* is a soprano; Caesar was sung by a soprano in Cavalli's *Eliogabalo*. In hundreds of other operas written before the mid-eighteenth century we find kings, great generals, famous heros, and assorted other male characters sung by sopranos and altos.

The explanation is that each of these roles was written for a type of singer now extinct, the *castrato* (plural, *castrati*), a male singer who had been subjected to castration at an early age and as a result had retained a treble voice into adulthood. Castrati grew to normal stature, and since they were males they sang male roles, even though their voices were soprano or alto. If we can trust the judgment of contemporary critics, they were the most spectacular singers in the entire history of opera; their voices were powerful, flexible, expressive, with a quality nothing at all like that of a boy soprano or a female soprano. They dominated opera for over a century, and the names of some of them—Farinelli, Senesino, Caffarelli—appear at the top of any list of the great singers of all time.

Composers made less use of castrati as the eighteenth century waned, and in the first decades of the nineteenth century they disappeared from opera altogether, although one lingered on long enough to make several phonograph recordings. They are now completely extinct, and we can no longer perform in any satisfactory way the operas written for them. There are attempts now and then, by schools and other small, noncommercial opera groups. Sometimes the roles written for castrati are sung by female sopranos and altos, which results in an impossible dramatic situation. The one opera with a castrato role which is still widely performed is Gluck's *Orfeo;* the role of Orpheus, written for an alto castrato, is done today by a mezzo or contralto dressed as a man. The other solution is to have the castrati parts sung an octave lower by a tenor or baritone, which at least results in male characters sung by male singers. But it violates the whole concept of sound. Such performances have not had enough appeal to warrant further revivals, at least on a commercial basis.

Perhaps this is just as well. We know from countless contemporary reports that a main delight of eighteenth-century opera was the ornamentation and improvisation of the good and great singers. The notes written down by Handel and his contemporaries were little more than a skeleton of what came out in performance. Since the tradition of florid singing and improvisation has died out, there is no way for us to reconstruct these operas in any satisfactory way for modern audiences.

SUMMARY

Even though no two operatic voices are exactly alike, voices are grouped into several types for convenience. The classification is according to range and quality. The coloratura soprano is the highest and most agile of all voices. Lyric and dramatic sopranos have about the same range but differ in quality; sometimes the term *spinto* is used for voices which have characteristics of both lyric and dramatic. Mezzo-sopranos have a slightly lower range and a heavier, darker sound. True contraltos are rare, and there is no sharp distinction between mezzo and contralto roles.

Lyric and dramatic tenors correspond to lyric and dramatic sopranos, and with tenors too the term *spinto* is sometimes used. There is also a strong tendency to group tenors according to nationality. Baritones, bass-baritones, and basses are the lower male voices.

Composers decide which types of voices to use for the various characters in their operas on the basis of several operatic conventions. Normally the parts of older persons are sung by lower voices, younger persons by the higher voices. The decision may also be made on the basis of the personality of the character to be cast. Deep male voices are most often used for imposing, impressive, powerful characters who hold positions of nobility or authority. The medium-range male voices—baritone and dramatic tenor—are frequently used for virile, positive characters, while lyric tenors are often cast as young lovers, poets, and other gentle people. The highest soprano voices are sometimes used to suggest nervous, flighty characters, and low female voices have been used for sinister, ominous parts.

Tastes in voices change. The castrati, male sopranos and altos, were once the most popular of all singers, but have completely disappeared from opera. Voices never before used in opera, children's voices and the countertenor, have been used in recent years.

WORDS AND MUSIC:
CONCEPTS AND DEFINITIONS

The word comes first in an opera. The text which the composer sets to music is called a *libretto*, or sometimes *book*, and he has this in hand before he begins to write his music. The word comes first in another sense, also: most librettists, at least up until the present century, have understood opera thoroughly, have known the conventions of operatic composition and structure, and have understood that if they wrote certain types of passages in their libretti, these would be set to a certain type of music by any composer. Thus the musical structure of an opera was largely determined by the librettist, before the composer ever began his job.

This point is dimly understood by American audiences, who for over a century have endured performances of operas in languages which they do not understand, and who consequently have been forced to listen to and think of opera as a purely musical form. Opera is unique precisely because it combines two arts, music and drama. Sometimes it becomes almost pure music, sometimes almost pure drama—but usually whatever happens at a given moment is somewhere between the two. A thread that will run through this entire book is the notion that the music of any section of an opera is determined to a greater or lesser degree by the structure and content of the section of text being set, and that any understanding of opera must begin by facing up to this fact.

A composer may set a passage of text in any one of a number of ways. This preliminary chapter will discuss the various types of text setting available to him, and suggest in each instance those considerations which determine his choice.

To begin with, a composer may do nothing at all to certain lines of text, and have them delivered by his singers as spoken dialogue. When lines of text are spoken without accompaniment, they are delivered just as they would be in a spoken drama.

PAPAGENO: Why do you stare at me so suspiciously?

TAMINO: Well, I—I was wondering whether you are a human being or not.

PAPAGENO: What was that?

TAMINO: Considering those feathers covering you, you look rather— (*approaches him.*)

PAPAGENO: Not like a bird, by any means? Stay away from me, I tell you, and don't trust me, because I have the strength of a giant. (*To himself:*) If he doesn't begin to be afraid of me soon, I shall have to run for it.

TAMINO: Strength of a giant? (*Looks at the serpent.*) Then perhaps it was you who saved me, and fought this poisonous snake?

PAPAGENO: Snake? (*Trembling, draws back a few steps.*) Is it dead or alive? [1]

The text is inflected, rises and falls in pitch within a narrow range, for reasons of comprehension and emphasis and character portrayal, but this inflection will vary from actor to actor (or director to director), and is in no way dictated by the composer. The lines will be spoken at a certain tempo, or rate of speed, but this tempo also will vary from actor to actor, perhaps even from performance to performance with the same actor. The lines will have rhythmic shape, dictated by the natural accentuation of the prose or poetry contained in them. And the lines will be delivered at a certain volume, which likewise will vary with different actors and directors. The composer who leaves lines completely without music retains no control over matters of inflection, tempo, rhythm, and volume.

The decision to have certain lines spoken, not sung, is made for dramatic reasons. For example, if a composer finds stretches of nonpoetic dialogue in his libretto, sections of exposition which do not suggest any particular musical treatment and which would not be clarified or intensified by the addition of any sort of music, he may choose to have these lines spoken. It is difficult to imagine any

[1] Mozart, *The Magic Flute*, Act I. Translation by Edward J. Dent. Published by Oxford University Press.

contribution that music could make to passages of libretto such as this:

JAQUINO: But Marcelline.—

MARCELLINE: Not a word! not a syllable! I'll not listen any longer to all your love nonsense about dying and sighing; so there's an end of it!

JAQUINO: Well who'd have thought it! Once it was "dear Jaquino" this, and "dear Jaquino" that! who had to heat the iron for you, and fold the linen, and take parcels to the prisoners— in fact, do all that an honest maid allows an honest lad to do for her. But ever since that Fidelio—It was I.

MARCELLINE: *(interrupting)* I don't deny it, I did like you then. But, look here, I'll be perfectly plain spoken with you; I liked you, but I wasn't in love with you. Fidelio attracts me far more. Between myself and him there is a far greater bond of sympathy.

JAQUINO: Sympathy indeed! with a young vagrant whom your father out of mere charity picked up at the gate—who—

MARCELLINE: *(angrily)* Who is poor and forsaken but who will yet be my husband! [2]

The use of spoken dialogue for passages of narration, usually in prose, is in part a matter of nationality; composers of operas in French, German, and English have made much more use of the technique than have composers setting Italian libretti. And it is much more common in comic operas than in tragic ones, more common in smaller "intimate" works than in large "grand" operas.

The most extensive use of spoken dialogue in opera can be found in comic operas of the eighteenth and nineteenth centuries: *Singspiel* in Germany, the *opéra-comique* in France, and the *ballad opera* in England. Spoken dialogue is also an important part of the *operetta* of the nineteenth and twentieth centuries, and of course of the *musical comedy* of the present century, which is very much a part of this subfamily of opera.

When sections of a libretto are delivered as spoken dialogue there is nothing to prevent complete comprehension of each word. If a composer feels that the understanding of certain words, phrases, and sentences of his text is absolutely essential to the development of his drama, he may elect to have these portions of the libretto spoken, rather than sung. Benjamin Britten, in his *Peter Grimes*, gets

[2] Beethoven, *Fidelio*, Act I. Translation by Percy Pinkerton.

along for several hours and most of three acts without using spoken dialogue, yet when he comes to what is in some ways the climax of his drama he abandons music altogether, briefly:

BALSTRODE: *(Crossing to lift Peter up)* Come on, I'll help you with the boat.
ELLEN: No!
BALSTRODE: Sail out till you lose sight of the Moot Hall. Then sink the boat. D'you hear? Sink her. Good-bye, Peter.
    There is a crunch of shingle as Balstrode leads Peter down to his boat, and helps him push it out. After a short pause, he returns, takes Ellen by the arm, and leads her away.[3]

Peter's fate having been made perfectly clear, the instructions to sink the boat given twice, Britten resumes with his music.

Likewise in Mascagni's *Cavalleria Rusticana*, the climactic fight between Alfio and Turiddu has taken place discreetly offstage. Santuzza remains on stage, awaiting news of the outcome; when a woman runs on, she speaks the words which tell of Turiddu's death, rather than singing them.

WOMAN: Hanno ammazzato compare Turiddu!

Most of the people who sit through performances of *Cavalleria Rusticana* in this country today have seen the opera before, or have at least read a synopsis of the story; they know how the fight will turn out, and it appears to be an unnecessary refinement for the composer to take such care to insure that these words be understood. The point that is so often missed by our contemporary commentators on opera is that almost every composer who has written opera has designed his works to have immediate dramatic appeal. The best operas have more than that—they have music strong enough to remain attractive after repeated hearings, and many operas have failed after spectacular triumphs when first performed simply because their music was too weak to stand familiarity. But the operas which we now consider the great works of the repertoire, the operas of Monteverdi and Gluck and Mozart and Verdi and Wagner and Berg and the like, made their initial strong impression as dramas, then became loved for their music as they became more familiar.

Occasionally a composer elects to have a certain key word,

[3] Britten, *Peter Grimes*, Act III. Copyright 1945 by Boosey & Hawkes, Ltd. Reprinted by permission.

phrase, or sentence spoken, not sung, because it is so charged with emotion as it stands that there is nothing left for music to add. Leoncavallo's *Pagliacci* ends with such a moment: Canio stands on the stage over the bodies of Nedda and Silvio, whom he has stabbed, in his clown outfit, and sobs out *"La commedia è finita!"* It is impossible to imagine this line sung—music at this moment could only detract from the powerfully melodramatic ending. The end of Menotti's *The Medium* is similar in effect: Baba looks into the face of Toby, whom she has just shot and who she would like to believe knows of a natural explanation for the apparently supernatural happenings which have unnerved her, and says "Was it you? Was it you?" Again it would be inconceivable for her to sing these lines. It is a telltale commentary on the structure of these operas that music becomes unnecessary at the very climax, but this fact cannot detract from the dramatic effectiveness of these moments.

Whatever the composer's reason for choosing to have spoken dialogue—to get over stretches of narrative, to insure that his audience understands a key moment in his drama, or admitting that his music can add nothing to certain lines of text—the result is that every word of the libretto can be comprehended in this part of his opera.

Many people believe that there is an impossible stylistic gap between spoken dialogue and song, that an opera which alternates between speech and song lacks the element of consistency essential to great works of art. Many directors faced with the problem of staging such a work attempt to narrow this gap by having the spoken lines delivered with even more stylization than would be acceptable on the legitimate stage; since the mere act of singing a text rather than speaking it is artificial, a convention, a stylization in itself, they believe that spoken lines can associate with sung lines only if they are made as artificial and stylized as possible. Many composers likewise acknowledge this gap and attempt to anticipate the director's problems by indicating themselves that their spoken dialogue is not to be uncontrolled speech but is to be restricted in some way, as in the following example from Carl Orff's *Der Mond*.[4]

DER WIRT
($\quad$ = 92)

Wo - zu die - net, wo - zu die - net, wo - zu die - net uns der Mond?

[4] Copyright 1939 by B. Schott's Sohne, Mainz. Assigned to Schott & Co. Ltd., London, 1947.

Here the composer controls the rhythm by indicating the relative duration of each syllable. He may also indicate the tempo at which the lines are to be spoken by the use of a time signature, and the volume by the use of a dynamic mark. The effect is still that of speech, but speech which has become more artificial than normal stage speech, speech which has become stylized through control of one or more of the elements of delivery.

Benjamin Britten, a successful contemporary English composer, has made much use of spoken dialogue in certain of his operas, and he sometimes feels uncomfortable enough about the jump from speech to song to do something about it. In the following example from his version of Gay and Pepusch's *The Beggars' Opera* he makes the transition by insinuating the orchestra in the course of a spoken line and having the performer go from speech to song by way of the intermediate step of declaimed speech with rhythm, tempo, and dynamics strictly prescribed.

Melodrama is a technical term in music, referring to the use of spoken dialogue against a musical accompaniment, as in the following example from Massenet's *Manon*.

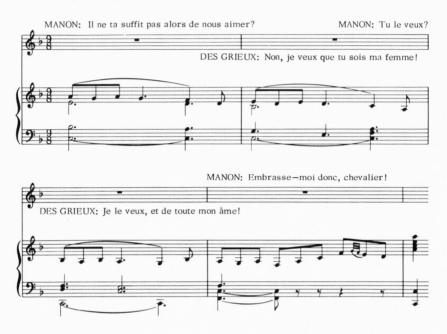

When a composer utilizes this device, he again leaves matters of inflection, tempo, rhythm, and volume up to his performers—with certain qualifications. The composer indicates that a certain amount of text is to be delivered in the time that a certain amount of music is played, and the singer may have to deliver the lines faster or slower than he would normally speak them on the stage, in order to come out with the music.

The performer has another element to contend with—the orchestra. When lines of text are being spoken against orchestral accompaniment there exists the possibility that words will be lost, either because of an unsatisfactory balance of dynamics or because the music coming from the pit is of enough interest to distract attention from the text. A composer generally selects for melodramatic treatment lines of text which he wants his audience to understand, but which will benefit from the things which music can do.

The effect of melodrama is quite different from that of spoken dialogue. Music, even the simplest music, has a magical ability to create moods, intensify emotions, underline significant words and phrases of a text. A composer often makes use of dialogue because he is confronted with a stretch of nonemotional, nonpoetic text which may be necessary in the structure of the drama but which suggests no sort of musical treatment. The sections of text treated as melodrama, on the other hand, are generally moments of high drama, pathos, or sentimentality, lines of text which must be understood and which can be made even more dramatic, pathetic, or sentimental by clever use of music.

One of the classic examples of melodrama in opera occurs near the beginning of the third act of Verdi's *La Traviata*. The situation is melodramatic to the hilt: the once glamorous courtesan Violetta Valery is dying of consumption (the doctor has just informed her maid and the audience that she has only a few hours to live). Parted from her lover Alfredo Germont as a result of a noble act of self-denial on her part, she re-reads a letter from his father which has given her hope during the past dark days.

> You have kept your promise. The duel took place; the Baron was wounded but is improving. Alfredo is abroad; I have told him of your sacrifice. He will return to you to ask your pardon; I will come too. Get well—you deserve a better future.
>
> Georgio Germont [5]

The letter contains information which the audience needs in order to follow the drama; until it is read there has been no word as to the outcome of the duel, and the audience does not know that Violetta has reason to hope for Alfredo's return. Quite aside from revealing necessary information, there is poignancy in this brief episode of the reading of the letter, poignancy which would come out if the text were simply recited but which is intensified by Verdi's treatment of the scene as melodrama. As Violetta reads, the strings of the orchestra quietly give out a melody which has been heard earlier in the opera during happier scenes between Violetta and Alfredo. The effect of the scene is remarkably stronger than could be created by either the text or the music, taken separately.

When treated sensitively and sparingly, melodrama can create certain moods and effects unobtainable by any other means, but if it is not handled carefully by both composer and performer the results can be mawkish and even ludicrous. Radio, moving pictures, and television depend regularly on melodrama, and each of the three

[5] Translation by Natalia Macfarren.

gives us daily examples of misuse of the device. It is interesting that in common parlance the word *melodramatic* has come to mean something excessively and cheaply dramatic, something sensational bordering on poor taste.

❧ RECITATIVE

The simplest type of text setting in which all elements of the singer's delivery are specified by the composer is known as recitative. The composer notates the exact rhythm, tempo, and volume, and also the precise pitches on which each syllable is to be sung, these normally remaining within a limited range.

In the simplest type of recitative, a single keyboard instrument (harpsichord, piano, organ) strikes occasional chords and the singer "recites" against this thin accompaniment. Some stringed bass instrument may play along with the keyboard, giving a firmer bass to each chord. This is commonly known as *secco recitative* (*secco* from the Italian, meaning *dry*), and is illustrated by the example from Mozart's *Così fan Tutte* on the opposite page.

Recitative is normally syllabic, with a single note of music for each syllable of text. If the language in which the opera is written is one spoken with a great deal of inflection—such as Italian, which is often described as a "musical" language in its spoken forms—and if the composer has understood the natural inflection and rhythm of this language well enough to imitate in his recitative its normal rise and fall, its accentuation and its long and short syllables, his recitative, even though sung at specific pitches, will sound not far removed from the spoken language. A singer with an intimate knowledge of the language may take the composer's indications of pitch, tempo, and the like as approximations, departing from them in order to make his delivery more like the spoken language. Recitative and spoken dialogue appear to be two altogether different things on paper, but highly stylized spoken delivery and freely interpreted recitative can turn out to be very nearly the same thing in performance.

Music is used in melodrama to create moods, to intensify emotions suggested by the text—in short, its purpose is to be expressive. Curiously enough, much recitative is not intended by the composer to be expressive, even though it represents a complete musical setting of the text. The performer sings the text, but the vocal line of much recitative (particularly in Italian opera) rises and falls within a narrowly limited range according to a few stereotyped patterns which are in no way altered by any particular text. The accompaniment is nothing more than a few sustaining or punctuating chords, which harmonically are the primary triads of the key in which the recitative begins and of related keys. Such an accompaniment is noncommittal expressively and serves only to keep the singer on pitch and provide the semblance of continuous music throughout the opera. Composers do not intend such recitative to be of any musical interest—many of them have allowed their students to write the recitatives to their operas —and a person who is forced to listen to such sections musically because of his unfamiliarity with the language is listening to opera in a way that no one, least of all the composer, ever intended.

The stylized, noncommittal recitative found in Italian opera of the seventeenth and eighteenth centuries and imitated in opera in other countries and at other times plays the same part in the structure of opera as does spoken dialogue in opera of another sort: it allows stretches of text to be delivered without interference from music. It is the text which counts, and music is present only because composers sensed that their operas would have greater stylistic unity if music of one sort or another ran throughout them. Even though an intelligent singer will modify the indicated rhythms and pitches of this sort of recitative to make his delivery more like the spoken language, the transition to more melodic singing is not nearly as abrupt as is the transition from spoken dialogue to singing.

Recitative need not be noncommittal; it can be made expressive. A composer may break away from the usual routine harmonies used in recitative and introduce unexpected dissonant or chromatic chords to emphasize and intensify certain key words or phrases. In the following example from Monteverdi's *Orfeo*, taken from the scene in which the messenger announces to Orfeo the death of his bride Euridice, the abrupt shift from the key of E major to distant minor chords somberly underlines the messenger's words "*è morta.*"

A composer may break away from the usual syllabic setting of recitative (one note of music for each syllable of text) by treating key words or phrases in a florid or melismatic way. This likewise has the effect of emphasizing or underlining the words so set, as in this fragment from Purcell's *Dido and Aeneas.*

Single words or even groups of words may be made more emphatic by a departure from the usual medium range in which recitative is sung. Use of extreme registers of the voice can intensify certain emotions suggested in the text: the extreme low register of most voices sounds dark, relaxed, somber, even menacing, while the top notes may sound bright, exciting, tense, strident, determined, or fierce. Stravinsky uses this technique to underline a key word in the following fragment of recitative from *The Rake's Progress*.[6]

Recitative accompanied by instruments of the orchestra other than a single keyboard and a stringed bass is referred to as *recitativo accompagnato, recitativo stromentato,* or, in English, simply *accompanied recitative*. There are several reasons why a composer may prefer this to secco recitative.

Some composers have felt that the transition from secco recitative, with its thin accompaniment of a single keyboard instrument, to sections using part of or all of the orchestra is disturbing itself. Gluck, writing of his aims in the Dedication of his *Alceste* (1769), said that in this opera he had used accompanied recitative rather than secco in order "that the concerted instruments . . . be introduced in proportion to the interest and intensity of the words, and not leave that sharp contrast between the aria and the recitative in the dialogue. . . ." Secco recitative disappeared for the whole of the nineteenth century, only to reappear in the twentieth.

Or the composer may use his orchestra to make recitative more expressive. The sound of the single keyboard instrument used to accompany secco recitative is unimpressive, particularly when the opera is performed in a large hall, as well as having a severely limited dynamic and tonal range. The use of various instruments of the orchestra in recitative gives much more variety of tonal color and volume. The following bit of recitative is taken from the scene in the first act of Mozart's *Don Giovanni* in which Donna Anna has just recognized the Don as the murderer of her father. The librettist has planned this as recitative—it contains essential information which must be gotten across to the audience—but Mozart sensed that the sound of ordinary secco recitative would not do justice to the surprise and anguish which Donna Anna feels at this moment. The solution was to set it as accompanied recitative, using most of his orchestra to back up the singer with a forceful accompaniment more in keeping with the mood of the scene.

When such expressive means are used in recitative, the effect is quite different from that of the routine recitative found in much Italian opera. Accompanying music plays much the same role it does in melodrama, creating moods and intensifying words and phrases of the text without obstructing it in any way. The contemporary composer Menotti, in his "A Note on the Lyric Theatre" written at the

The famous bass Ezio Pinza as Mozart's Don Giovanni.

time of the first performances of his successful opera *The Consul,*
says:

> For the contemporary composer the exciting challenge is the
> recitative. It is the logical instrument of action, and he must
> find the way to make it work for him musically and dramat-
> ically. He is immediately more fortunate than the prose
> playwright, of course, in possessing the wonderful medium
> of music, which can make its point so much more quickly
> than pages of words. With a single, well-written musical
> phrase, he can convey the most delicate relationships of
> character and establish the most elusive abstract emo-
> tions. . . . Much of the text of "The Consul" depends upon
> quick-paced dialogue, and I know now that the sections
> which pleased me most are those in which I feel those
> nervous little passages are successfully integrated.[7]

The following example, taken from the end of the first scene of the
second act of *The Consul,* shows what can be done with recitative
by expressive use of harmony, rhythm, dynamics, range, and orchestration.[8]

Expressive, accompanied recitative can be so flexible and so
effective a tool that whole scenes and even a few entire operas have
utilized this method of text setting to the exclusion of all others.
The very earliest operas, the works of the Florentine Camerata, make
almost exclusive use of "inflected speech," the singers delivering the

[7] From the New York *Herald Tribune,* March 12, 1950. Reprinted by permission.

[8] Copyright 1950 by G. Schirmer, Inc.

Allegro

told you . . . I can-not pos-sib-ly get all those doc-u-ments you want

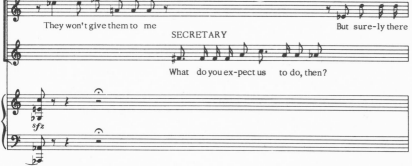

They won't give them to me

SECRETARY

But sure-ly there

What do you ex-pect us to do, then?

must be a way you can help me.

Doc-u-ments or no doc-u-ments,

I must get a-way.

text in mostly syllabic fashion with key words and passages made more expressive by melodic turns, vocal ornamentation, and subtle harmonic progressions. And in Debussy's *Pelléas et Mélisande*, written three centuries later, singers declaim their texts within a narrow range, supported by a large but quiet and delicate orchestra.

For the performer, problems of projecting the text are minor in most recitative. In secco recitative, with only the single keyboard instrument to contend with, singers with even modest means have no difficulty in being heard over the accompaniment, and most operatic composers have understood the necessity of treating their orchestra with great care in accompanied recitative. If the composer has set his text with close attention to proper rhythm and inflection, there should be no difficulty in getting it across to the audience, provided the singer has not had the misfortune of studying with a teacher who believes in distorting vowel sounds and ignoring consonants for the sake of a "pure" sound. A composer may run into difficulty, though, if he is not careful in his use of extreme registers of the voice. A singer with no congenital or acquired vocal problems should have no difficulty in singing so that the text can be understood in his middle register, assuming that the text has been well set by the composer and the performer has a satisfactory knowledge of the language being sung. Likewise tenors and baritones usually have no trouble projecting a text when they are singing in their high, even highest, register. But a tenor descending to what is for him a low register begins to have trouble getting words out clearly, as will a baritone or a bass singing near the bottom of his range. All female voices have the same difficulty in their lowest registers, and the problem becomes acute at the top: even the best-intentioned and best-trained sopranos, altos, contraltos, mezzos, and coloraturas begin losing words the higher they sing, and when the top of their range is approached it makes no difference what language the composer has set. This is not the place to discuss the physical and psychological causes of this readily observed phenomenon, but merely to point out that even though comprehensibility in extreme ranges varies with the particular language being sung and with particular vowels and consonants, the highest reaches of female voices (and to a lesser extent the lower registers of all voices) are useless for getting words across.

If a composer decides to strengthen the impact of a certain section of text by having a voice sing quite high or quite low he must do this in a certain way, or else he may lose his text and with it the whole point of the passage. He may achieve the effect by having critical words sung on higher or lower notes than those which surround it, high or low enough to create the effect of a change of range but not extreme enough to go beyond the range of comprehension. He may choose his spots carefully and use extreme range only for those voices that can project a text in such a register. He may have extremes of range fall on words which are unimportant and do not need to be heard in order for the sense of the passage to come across. Or he may make use of text repetition, a classic operatic device, having the same words or equivalent ones precede or follow the words which may not be understood because of the range in which they are sung.

A special sort of recitative, called *sprechstimme*, has been used by a number of composers in this century since Arnold Schoenberg introduced it in his *Pierrot Lunaire* (1912) and *Gurre-Lieder* (first performed in 1913). The composer notates, precisely, the rhythm in which the text is to be recited, the tempo at which the music is to move, and the volume; he also notates the rise and fall of the vocal line, using *x*'s rather than the usual noteheads. This example is from the first scene of the third act of Alban Berg's *Wozzeck*.[9]

The tradition of the performance of *sprechstimme* is that pitches and intervals between syllables are not precise. The individual performer delivers the lines at a pitch level which is comfortable or expressive, preferably somewhere in the neighborhood of the notated pitch; if the composer has indicated a rising inflection from one syllable to the next, the performer must follow this contour, if not the exact interval. Pitch is not maintained for the duration of the syllable, as in singing, but may rise, fall, waver, or decrease in volume before the following syllable is spoken. The effect of *sprechstimme* is of exaggerated, artificial delivery of text, no longer speech but yet not quite singing.

[9] Reprinted with permission of Universal Edition A. G., Vienna.

ARIOSO

At times a composer setting a portion of text as recitative will find something in this text or in the musical material he has been using which suggests a melodic development more extensive than is usual in recitative. A melodic fragment may be attractive enough to make him want to allow it to unfold sequentially for a while, or to work up to a small climax; or the composer may sense that a certain bit of text will be more expressive if given the benefit of a more complete musical statement. Composers are inconsistent in their use of terms; *arioso* has been used to designate several different types of text settings, but it is most often used for a brief section in which music is allowed to follow its own logic for a bit, to develop a musical idea of some interest, but not to become elaborate enough for a complete musical section. An arioso section of this sort is usually approached from recitative and may be followed by recitative; it may grow out of secco recitative and be accompanied only by a single keyboard instrument, or more commonly it may develop from accompanied recitative and thus have the advantage of orchestral accompaniment. Its effect is of a temporary heightening of musical interest in a section in which the text, or the text and the music working together, have been of primary interest. The following section of arioso is from Verdi's *Il Trovatore*.

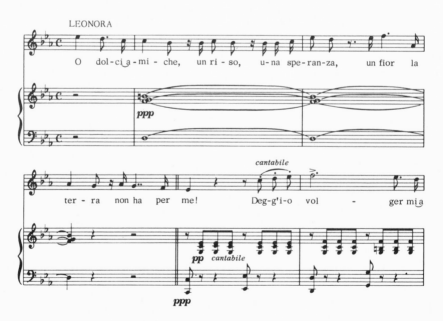

Quel che de-gli af-flit - ti è so - lo so-ste - gno

A composer may treat an entire section of what appears in the libretto as recitative in a more melodic way than usual. Composers of the era of Puccini were particularly fond of this technique. A passage set in this way is usually called an arioso, if the music does not take on a definite form.

In arioso sections, with music sometimes moving in directions dictated by purely musical considerations, there are more possible pitfalls for the composer who wants to project his text to his audience. For musical reasons, a composer may be tempted to use a larger and louder group of instruments than the average singer can compete with; his vocal line may want to flow to difficult registers of the human voice; a musical pattern may suggest that a certain note should ascend, despite the fact that the syllable on which this note is sung descends in normal inflection; his melodic line may persuade him to prolong a syllable which is naturally short.

ARIA AND SONG

In both recitative and arioso the text is of primary importance. The composer takes care that his music not interfere with the audience's comprehension of the words being sung, making it either so noncommittal that it does not draw attention to itself or expressive in ways directly related to the sense of the text. Abstract musical forms are not allowed to impose their particular patterns on the text; what form there is results from poetical forms already present in the libretto.

But these two types of music are by no means the whole story. There are many moments in most operas when musical interest is equal to, or even surpasses, the dramatic or poetic interest of the particular section of text being sung; often music is allowed to develop in its own way, to take on some form of its own. Such a section, when it is written for a solo singer, is called an aria.

Since the purpose and effect of an aria are quite different from those of any of the text-setting techniques already discussed, the form is likewise different. It is generally written in a self-contained, complete, rounded musical form similar to the forms used in purely instrumental music. It develops according to musical logic and works up to musical climaxes which may or may not coincide with climaxes implied in the text. In arioso and recitative music grows from text, but in an aria the words are frequently molded to fit what is happening in the music. Many arias can be separated from their parent operas and sung as recital pieces, making complete musical (if not always dramatic) sense. Audiences may listen to arias in exactly the way they listen to instrumental music: they may concentrate on the singer's voice, the tone quality, his ability to attain and sustain extremes of range and dynamics and get through difficult technical passages with ease and control, his ability to compete successfully with the orchestra and to project his voice into whatever auditorium is in use. This is not dissimilar to the way in which a music lover would listen to, say, a violinist playing a concerto. And just as the composer of a concerto gives the orchestra something interesting to do whenever the soloist is not playing, so an opera composer furnishes his orchestra with music of melodic, harmonic, or orchestral interest when there is a break in the vocal part.

It is possible to listen with interest to the music of many arias even when they are divorced from their text. A performance of a section of secco recitative in which a violin or trumpet substituted for the voice would be absurd and meaningless; an arioso section done by a flute might be attractive, but would not have enough musical form or development to sustain interest. But many arias could be and have been done successfully as instrumental and orchestral selections, even though taking them from their dramatic surroundings eliminates an important dimension.

There are various types and forms of aria, as will be pointed out in the next chapter. But a distinction must be made at this point between *song* and *aria*. Many operas contain sections for solo singers that are of modest proportions, largely syllabic, that generally avoid the extremes of vocal range, are lightly orchestrated, and are constructed as simple, symmetrical musical forms with straightforward, easily comprehended melodic lines. Such a section is often called a *song*, or *air*, or *Lied*, or *chanson*, and its effectiveness depends more on the charm and expressiveness of the music and the personality and musicianship of the singer than on spectacular virtuoso singing. The text setting is such that all, or almost all, of the words can be understood, yet the music has structure and independent substance itself. It is possible for a composer to achieve perfect equilibrium between music and text in a song, with the two elements complementing one another in a way that is not possible in any other sort of text setting.

Certain types of opera make almost exclusive use of song, rather than more elaborate arias: the English ballad opera and the French opéra-comique of the eighteenth century, the operetta of the nineteenth century, and the musical comedy of the present day. In other operas song is used for variety, to contrast with other types of arias in which the composer has challenged his singers by writing complex, highly ornamented melodic lines often moving into the extreme registers of the voice.

As opera is understood in this country today, arias are the supreme moments. Audiences suffer through spoken dialogue and melodrama and various sorts of recitative, sustained only by anticipation of arias to come. Many directors tailor their productions to this taste by shortening or even eliminating stretches of recitative or dialogue and by staging works to make it clear that they are interested only in the arias. Recording companies have issued discs with all recitative eliminated, leaving an opera nothing more than a string of arias and ensembles.

CONCLUSION

If opera were a musical form, as the American public has been led to believe, there would be no excuse whatsoever for secco recitative, melodrama, declamation, and other such methods of dealing with a text. But opera is not a musical form, it is a musical-dramatic form, and the composer's choice of method of text setting is almost always dictated by dramatic, not musical, considerations. Listening to the music alone will seldom give a hint as to why a composer chose to set part of his text as arioso, part as recitative, part as aria. His decision is made on the basis of the text, of knowing just what the various types of settings would add to or detract from it, of choosing the means that will most enrich each dramatic situation. Composers of all centuries have understood opera in this way, as an art form in which the text generates various types of music. Audiences in other countries are still able to participate in an opera performance in this way. American audiences cannot, and as long as they cannot they will be unable to comprehend opera as composers have always wanted it to be comprehended. Recitative and melodrama are of less musical interest than most arias, certainly, but a person who does not understand why a composer makes use of the various techniques of text setting is oblivious to one of the things that make up opera.

III

RECITATIVE AND ARIA

Most historians agree that opera began in Florence at the end of the sixteenth century, among a group of poets, musicians, and dilettantes who called themselves the *Camerata*. In their meetings, held in the palace of Count Bardi, they discussed ancient Greek music and drama; they convinced themselves that Greek dramas had been sung, but that music served the function of intensifying and clarifying the text without in any way calling attention to itself. After much preliminary discussion and work, members of the group produced several works right at the turn of the century which are generally considered to be the first operas: *Dafne* (1597), with a libretto by Rinuccini and music by Peri; *Euridice* (1600) by Rinuccini and Caccini; and another *Euridice* in the same year with music by Peri. These works were performed for a small, select audience of intelligent and well-educated people, in a room in the palace. A small orchestra, out of sight behind screens, played unobtrusive accompaniments to the vocal lines, which fluctuated between what we today would call accompanied recitative and arioso.

Here, at the birth of opera, there was no hint of recitative and aria. There was no need for it. These men thought of their operas as dramas, with music playing a completely subordinate role. Musical resources were kept at a minimum in the vocal lines and in the accompaniment; the text had been designed to be comprehensible on first hearing; the singers, many of them amateurs, had been impressed with the necessity of projecting their texts as clearly as possible.

Thus audiences at these first performances were able to follow every line of the text, just as in spoken drama.

But opera spread. Better composers began writing in this new form, men who had the ability to write music of great interest in itself. Performances were no longer in such intimate surroundings, but in larger halls. Much larger orchestras were used. The best singers of the day were attracted to opera. For all of these reasons there was a trend to the use of more elaborate music: composers wanted their music to play a more prominent part than it had in the earliest operas, more sound was needed to fill the larger halls, singers wanted music which would display their vocal techniques to greater advantage. There arose for the first time the basic conflict between music and drama and the first attempts to solve it by some sort of alternation of the two; these attempts eventually led to recitative-aria structures, and almost all later opera was based on this principle or on some modification of it. Even the operas of such "reform" composers as Gluck and Wagner, who preached the union of music and drama, depended much more than the composers were willing to admit on this most basic of all operatic techniques.

THE METASTASIAN IDEAL

Pietro Metastasio (1698–1782) is well known to students of Italian literature; handsome editions of his works are in print, and no course in the history of Italian poetry and drama would be complete without readings and discussions of his works.

Metastasio was almost certainly the greatest librettist in the entire history of opera, but from the vantage point from which the present century has chosen to view it, this counts for very little. His name is encountered in books devoted to the general history of music only in footnotes, if at all, and recent histories of opera pay little more attention to him. This is a curious situation, since his literary fame rests almost entirely on his opera libretti.

Coming at the end of a period of over a century in which writers had wrestled with the peculiar problems of opera, Metastasio's libretti represent a highly successful solution. The plots deal with kings and other heroic characters of ancient history, there are generally six characters in the cast, and the three acts are each made up of from six to fifteen or more scenes. Each scene, with few exceptions, is constructed in a way which makes sense only when it is remembered that we are dealing with a libretto, not a spoken drama: one, two, or more of the characters speak, their conversation moving the plot forward to a point of emotional crisis, whereupon one of the characters is given a short poem elaborating on the emotional state in which he has been placed.

The following scene (Act II, scene 3) from Metastasio's *La Clemenza di Tito* (first performed in Vienna on November 4, 1734, with music by the composer Caldara) illustrates this structure.

ARGENE: Ah! tell me, princess, is there under Heaven
One, O ye powers! more hopeless than myself?
ARISTEA: Yes, Argene, that wretch am I!
ARGENE: O never
May love on thee inflict the pangs I feel!
Thou knows't not what I've lost; how dear the heart
Had cost me, which thou now hast ravish'd from me.
ARISTEA: Nor cans't thou judge the torments I endure.

    I grant the sufferings great you prove,
    You lose the object of your love;
    But yet may freely vent your grief,
    And seek from pity some relief:
    While I, by ruthless Fortune crest,
    Behold myself and lover lost;
    Yet cannot, midst my woes, retain
    The wretched freedom to complain[1]

Characters come and go. Occasionally there is a direction as to how a line should be delivered, or to whom, but Metastasio does not depend on stage action to clarify what is happening—everything essential to an understanding of the plot and of the personalities of the characters is contained in the words they speak.

Metastasio, himself a musician and composer, had frequent and cordial contacts with the operatic composers who used his libretti and with the singers who performed in these operas. He knew, as every successful librettist has known, that the structure of his libretto would determine the structure of the music. He knew that a composer setting the scene just quoted to music would set the first part in recitative, probably the simplest sort of secco recitative, and the concluding brief poem as an aria. He knew that he himself, in his libretto, was writing recitative and aria. Thus a typical Metastasian

[1] Translation by John Hoole—1800.

scene came out, musically, as a section of secco recitative followed by an aria, and a typical act came out, musically, as a chain of recitative-aria scenes.

In spoken dramas scenes sometimes end with soliloquies in which one character speaks at length about things which trouble or please him, but it would be curious and unnecessary for a play to be built of a succession of such scenes. In opera it is necessary; this is the whole point of the Metastasian libretto. Although Italian is frequently said to be a "musical" language, even the Italian composer has to face up to the problem of not having his text understood if he uses too elaborate musical means. The recitative-aria pattern of a typical Metastasian scene affords him a satisfactory solution. In the first part of the scene, devoted to narrative or dialogue which moves the plot forward to a moment of emotional crisis, he uses secco recitative, a type of setting in which musical means are so modest as not to interfere with comprehension of the text or to call attention to themselves. At the point where the dramatic situation has been clearly drawn, the librettist furnishes him with a short poem dealing with a single emotion, and the composer is free to use more elaborate musical means, even if these result in the loss of some of the text. If he sets the first line or two of the aria in such a way that the text can be understood, and if a few words and phrases come through later, the audience will know all that it needs to know and can devote most of its attention to the beauty of the singer's voice and to the arpeggios, trills, ornamentation, or high notes with which the aria is sprinkled, or which the singer is expected to add.

The principle underlying this type of libretto, then, is that passages of narration and action, in which all essential information is given and in which the dramatic crises occur, alternate with passages of contemplation and reflection. This narration-contemplation or action-reflection pattern results in a recitative-aria structure in the music.

We are told that singers of Metastasio's time often substituted an aria from another opera for the aria furnished by librettist and composer, and critics of the Metastasian era of opera have cited this practice as evidence of the inferior dramatic nature of these works. But a Metastasio libretto is constructed in such a way that the dramatic structure would be intact even if *all* the arias were replaced, or even eliminated. Arias elaborate on one of a rather limited number of emotional states—jealousy, hopeless love, faith, and the like—and no violence is done to the drama if another aria of similar sentiment is substituted or if the aria is omitted. It is only when the *recitative* is tampered with that the dramatic structure is weakened or destroyed.

Reading through a Metastasio libretto, one might think that the work is mostly made up of recitative, with an occasional aria. But one has the opposite impression from hearing a performance of an opera based on such a libretto. Recitative is treated so simply and gotten over so quickly, and the arias are given such elaborate musical settings, that the effect is of a succession of arias linked together by recitative. In the following scene from Metastasio's *Il Re Pastore* (Act I, scene 5) recitative and aria seem to be of equal length.

TAMIRI: No, voi non siete, o Dei,
Quanto fin or credei,
Inclementi con me. Cangiaste, è vero,
In capanna il mio soglio, in rozzi velli
La porpora real: ma fido ancora
L'idol mio ritrovai.
Pietosi Dei, voi mi lasciaste assai.

Di tante sue procelle
Già si scordò quest'alma;
Già ritrovò la calma
Sul volto del mio ben.

Fra l'ira delle stelle
Se palpitò d'orrore,
Or di contento il core
Va palpitando in sen.

In Mozart's setting of this libretto (K 208), written in Salzburg in 1775, the recitative portion of the scene is gotten over in 10 measures of the simplest possible music.

The aria is introduced by 21 measures in the orchestra, then the voice commences with a syllabic setting of the first lines of the text, soon moving on to highly melismatic treatment, which continues

Allegro aperto

TAMIRI

già ri - tro - vò la— cal - ma

sul vol - to del mio ben, già—

— ri-tro-vò la— cal - - - -

- - - ma— sul— vol - to— del— mio ben.

for 109 measures, making a total of 130 measures for the vocal-instrumental setting of the aria text. The recitative should be sung in about thirty seconds and the aria should take almost five minutes.

Both before and after the Metastasian era, operatic structure was more flexible, and relief from the unvarying succession of recitative-aria, action-reflection scenes was obtained in various ways which will be discussed later. But in opera of almost all periods, no matter how complex the structure of the libretto and the resulting music, recitative-aria patterns persist as one of the basic means of organization and one of the most successful solutions to the fundamental operatic problem of balancing musical and dramatic interest.

Many later operas are full of recitative-aria patterns which work in the same way as those just discussed. In the following scene from Mozart's *Don Giovanni* (libretto by Lorenzo Da Ponte) a brief section of narration, set as secco recitative, leads to a more extended section of contemplation, set as an aria. Libretto and music work together, complementing and reinforcing one another just as in the operas of Metastasio.

DON OTTAVIO:
'Tis indeed past believing that a crime so atrocious was
    the act of a man of breeding!
I must relax no effort till I know what the truth is.
To my beloved I have a duty, I've a duty to my friend
    Don Giovanni;
Yes, I must undeceive her, or else avenge her!

Mine be her burden, bravely to bear it,
Could she feel comfort, my heart would share it.
Her heart is bleeding, mine bleeds for her.
Sighs she for sorrow, her sighs inspire me,
Her righteous anger, her tears, too, fire me.
Could I not serve her, death I'd prefer.
Mine be her burden, bravely to bear it,
Could she feel comfort, my heart would share it.
Her heart is bleeding, mine bleeds for her.[2]

In some operas the action-reflection patterns of the libretto are treated by the composer as alternation of spoken dialogue and singing, rather than as recitative and aria. The following scene from Mozart's *The Magic Flute* is constructed in exactly the same way as the scene from *Don Giovanni*. But this is a German opera, a Singspiel,

[2] Translation by Edward J. Dent. Published by Oxford University Press.

and the narrative section is delivered in speech, not in recitative as in *Don Giovanni*, which is written in Italian and follows the conventions of Italian opera.

PAMINA: *(entering joyfully):* You here? Kindly Gods! I thank you. I heard the sound of your flute and I followed the tone swift as an arrow. But you are sad? You speak no word to your Pamina? *(Tamino sighs and motions her away.)* Do you love me no more? *(Tamino sighs again.)* Papageno, you tell me what troubles my friend. *(Papageno has his mouth full and motions her away:* Hm, hm, hm!) You too? Oh, this is worse than death! *(Pause.)* My dearest Tamino!

Ah, I feel, to grief and sadness,
    Ever turned is love's delight.
Gone forever joy and gladness,
    In my heart reigns mournful night.
See, Tamino, see my anguish,
    See my tears for thee, my own.
If for love thou dost not languish,
    Peace I find the death alone.[3]

This type of structure is one with which most Americans are familiar, from its use in musical comedy and operetta, which are direct descendants of Singspiel and opéra-comique. No matter how remote they may be in musical style from serious opera, many of the operatic techniques are the same. A scene such as the following, from Gilbert and Sullivan's *H.M.S. Pinafore*, works in just the same way as the preceding one from *Don Giovanni*.

BUTTERCUP: But tell me who's the youth whose falt'ring feet
    With difficulty bear him on his course?
BOATSWAIN: That is the smartest lad in all the fleet, Ralph Rackstraw!
BUTTERCUP: Ralph! That name! Remorse! Remorse!
    Enter Ralph from hatchway.

. . . . . .

RALPH: I know the value of a kindly chorus,
    But choruses yield little consolation
    When we have pain, and sorrow, too, before us!
    I love—and love, alas, above my station!
BUTTERCUP: He loves, and loves a lass above his station.

[3] Translation by Edward J. Dent. Published by Oxford University Press.

CHORUS: Yes, yes, the lass is much above his station.

RALPH: A maiden fair to see, the pearl of minstrelsy,
   A bud of blushing beauty;
  For whom proud nobles sigh, and with each other vie,
   To do her menial's duty.

  A suitor, lowly born, with hopeless passion torn,
   And poor, beyond denying,
  Has dared for her to pine, at whose exalted shrine,
   A world of wealth is sighing.

  Unlearned he in aught, save that which love has taught
   (For love has been his tutor);
  Oh, pity, pity me—our captain's daughter she;
   And I, that lowly suitor!

VARIATIONS: RECITATIVE

As successful as the action-reflection, recitative-aria structure has been, many composers have found it too inflexible, too confining, too symmetrical, too arbitrary. For many composers, and for certain audiences, the constant shift from spoken dialogue or secco recitative to aria, from a section with no music whatsoever or with severely limited musical means to a section in which most or all of the orchestra plays against a melodic and often florid vocal part, results in a monotonously checkered pattern of sonority, a constant shifting from one type of sound to another. No sooner had Metastasian opera reached a peak of perfection than composers and librettists were wondering if other types of organization might not be preferable. Sonority was sometimes leveled off between recitative and aria by doing away with secco recitative and having recitative sections accompanied by part or all of the orchestra.

The following scene from the third act of Mozart's *The Marriage of Figaro* is constructed in the same way as the two Mozart recitative-aria scenes quoted above.

COUNTESS: Is Susanna not here? I'm impatient to be told what his lordship has said to her proposal. And yet I'm doubtful if it was not too bold; my lord is always so impulsive and so jealous. But what's the harm? I keep the assignation wearing Susanna's dress, while she wears mine, under cover of darkness. Oh, heavens, what a humiliation I suffer! Oh, cruel husband, to reduce me to this! Did ever woman have to bear such a life of neglect and desertion, such jealous fury, such insults? Once he lov'd me, then disdain'd me, and now betrays me; ah, so must I beg for a servant's favour?

I remember days long departed,
    Days when love no end could know;
I remember fond vows and fervent—
    All were broken long ago.

Oh, then why, if I was fated
    From that height of joy to fall,
Must I still those happy moments
    In my hour of pain recall?

Dare I hope to be rewarded?
    Must I languish all in vain?
Some day, surely, my devotion
    Might his faithless heart regain.[4]

As in the scenes from *Don Giovanni* and *The Magic Flute*, the libretto breaks into two parts, the first establishing an emotional situation and the second expounding on it. But whereas there was no musical continuity between the two sections in the two previously quoted scenes, here the recitative section is accompanied by the strings of the orchestra, and the aria is more a musical continuation of the first section than the beginning of something altogether different. This scene, though still a recitative-aria structure, is bound together by the sonority of the orchestra.

The desire to have more consistency of orchestral sound led composers of the nineteenth and twentieth centuries to abandon secco recitative altogether (although in a handful of recent operas it has been reintroduced); recitative in operas of these periods is accompanied by part or all of the orchestra, and the harpsichord has disappeared from the opera house except when it is used in revivals of older works.

Much accompanied recitative is similar, in treatment of the voice, to secco recitative. In the following scene from Benjamin Britten's *Peter Grimes*, the libretto suggests a recitative-aria scene just as strongly as any of the examples earlier in this chapter, and Britten has set the first section of the scene with the voices declaiming the text syllabically within a narrow range and with the orchestra doing little more than supplying a few chords. The second part is a florid aria, and the scene differs from a Metastasian recitative-aria

[4] Translation by Edward J. Dent. Published by Oxford University Press.

scene only in that the orchestra plays during the recitative section. The difference is one of sonority, not of treatment of text.

> *(Ellen and Balstrode walk up slowly from the beach, in earnest talk)*
>
> ELLEN: Is the boat in?
>
> BALSTRODE: Yes—for more than an hour. Peter seems to have disappeared. Not in his boat. Not in his hut.
>
> ELLEN: This I found, down by the tide-mark.
>
> *(B. shines his lantern on the boy's jersey, which Ellen holds out to him)*
>
> BALSTRODE: The boy's!
>
> ELLEN: My broidered anchor on the chest!
> Embroidery in childhood was a luxury of idleness.
> A coil of silken thread giving dreams of a silk and satin life.
> Now my broidery affords the clue whose meaning we avoid!
>
> My hand remembers its old skill—
> These stitches tell a curious tale.
> I remember I was brooding
> On the fantasies of children
> And dreamt that only by wishing
> I could bring some silk into their lives.
>
> Now my broidery affords the clue whose meaning we avoid.[5]

Often, however, a composer writing accompanied recitative will break away from the stylized, inexpressive patterns common to secco recitative. As noted in the last chapter, if a portion of his libretto suggests more dramatic or expressive treatment, he may take the voice up to an extreme range, treat it briefly in a melismatic fashion, or let it develop for a bit into a melody. In such a passage the musical contrast between recitative and aria becomes less marked and may even vanish altogether. The following scene from the last act of Puccini's *Madame Butterfly* is clearly a recitative-aria sequence in the libretto. The aria was designed to have great musical interest, and in fact has become one of the most popular of all operatic arias. But the first part of the scene, which looks like recitative in the libretto, is supplied with music which on occasion draws on vocal and instrumental resources equal to those used in the aria. The result is a much more extended musical unit than was possible (or desirable) in Metastasian opera.

[5] Copyright 1945 by Boosey & Hawkes, Ltd. Reprinted by permission.

BUTTERFLY: He'll return.

SUZUKI: Will he?

BUTTERFLY: Why did he order the Consul to provide this dwelling for us? Now answer that! And why was he so careful to have the house provided with safe locks, if he did not intend to come again?

SUZUKI: I do not know.

BUTTERFLY: You do not know? Then I will tell you. It was to keep outside those spiteful plagues, my relations, who might annoy me; and inside, it was to give me, his wife, protection—his beloved little wife, Butterfly.

SUZUKI: I have never heard of a foreign husband returning to his nest.

BUTTERFLY: Silence, or I'll kill you. Why, just before he went, I asked him, you'll come back again to me? And with his heart so heavy, to conceal his trouble, with a smile he answered: "O Butterfly, my tiny little child bride, I'll return with the roses, the warm and sunny season when the red-breasted robins are nesting." He will return.

SUZUKI: Let us hope so.

BUTTERFLY: Say it with me: he will return.

SUZUKI: He will return (she breaks into tears)

BUTTERFLY: You are weeping? Why? Why? You have no faith!
One fine day we'll notice a thread of smoke on the sea
On the far horizon,
And then the ship appearing;
Then the trim white vessel glides into the harbor, and fires
    her cannon in a salute.
Do you see?
Now he is coming!
I do not go to meet him. Not I!
I stay upon the brow of the hill,
And wait there . . . and wait for a long time,
But never weary of the long waiting.
From out of the crowded city a man is coming,
A little speck in the distance, climbing the hill.
Can you guess who it is?
And when he reaches the summit, can you guess what
    he'll say?
He'll call: "Butterfly" from the distance.
I, without answering, remain hidden,
A bit to tease him and a bit so as not to die
At our first meeting;
And then, a little troubled, he will call:

"Dear child-wife of mine, dear little orange blossom!"
The names he used to call me when he came here.

It will all happen as I have been telling it to you.
Banish your idle fears,
He will return,
I know it.[6]

It is in the nature of art that there is no final solution to any problem. Metastasio's art, in its symmetry, restraint, and perfection of form, is classical; other composers and librettists have had the desire to create works more complex in form, more vivid in emotion, and with more interplay of emotional states.

A common modification of the recitative-aria structure replaces the pattern of narration-elaboration with a more flexible and complex combination of the two elements. A single scene may contain several sections of recitative, each leading to an emotional crisis which is commented on in aria or arioso; or an aria may be interrupted by recitative, in which new information is offered, after which the aria continues in another vein. Recitative and aria have the same functions as before, but they are used more freely in the construction of a longer and more complex scene.

The second act of Carl Maria von Weber's *Der Freischütz* contains a justly celebrated scene, sometimes referred to as a recitative and aria (*"Leise, leise"*), but actually built on free interplay between the two elements. The scene takes place in the home of Cuno, head forester of the Duke of Bohemia, whose daughter Agatha has fallen in love with Max, a young forester. Agatha is alone in her room; it is evening. The scene begins with recitative.

AGATHA: Sleep came to me so easily before I saw him.
Yes, love and sorrow seem always to go hand in hand.
I wonder if the moon will smile on his path?
(*She draws the curtain at the window*)
What a beautiful night!

She goes out on the balcony and begins an aria.

AGATHA: Softly, softly, blessed melody,
Soar to the stars.
Resound, my song, and float
My prayer to the gates of heaven.

[6] Translation by R. H. Elkin.

Though the aria has scarcely begun, it breaks off into recitative.

AGATHA: Oh, how bright the golden stars are, glowing with such a pure gleam; But there, over the distant mountains, a storm seems to be gathering, and there in the woods a host of dark and heavy clouds is drifting.

After this interruption, the aria continues.

AGATHA: I raise my hands to you,
      God without beginning or end.
  Send your angels
      To protect us from danger.

The aria continues, but with a change of key, meter, and tempo.

AGATHA: Rest has settled over everything!
      My beloved, why do you tarry?
  My ear also listens eagerly,
      But I hear nothing but the rustling of the treetops,
  Nothing but the whispering of the birches in the forest
      Breaking the profound stillness.

Again there is a shift back to recitative.

AGATHA: Only the nightingale and the cricket break the stillness
      of the night air.
  But what was that! Did my ear deceive me?
  There was a sound like a footstep,
  Something is coming through those pines!

Recitative is no longer adequate to express her excitement; so there is a shift to arioso.

AGATHA: It is he! It is he!
  I must give him a signal!
  Your sweetheart has been watching for you in the night!
  (she waves her handkerchief to him)

Once again back to recitative.

AGATHA: He does not seem to see me yet.
  Heavens! unless the moonlight is deceiving my eyes he is wearing a wreath of flowers in his hat! That must mean that he made the best shot;

Again, as her emotions become more intense, there is a shift to arioso.

AGATHA: That promises well for tomorrow!
Oh, sweet hope! revived courage!

The dramatic situation is now quite different from what it was at the beginning of the scene, and her music is now different in mood, tempo, melody, and in every other way.

AGATHA: My pulse pounds and my heart boils,
I feel a sweet enchantment towards him!
Could I dare to hope that it could be . . .
Yes, fate is turning for my beloved,
Who will prove himself to be true tomorrow!

And once again there is a shift to recitative.

AGATHA: Is it deception? Is it an illusion?
Heaven, accept the thanks of my heart for this ray of hope.

And the aria continues and brings the scene to a conclusion.

AGATHA: Heaven, accept the thanks of my heart
For this ray of hope.
My pulse pounds and my heart boils,
I feel a sweet enchantment.

Though this scene utilizes recitative to convey information and aria to rhapsodize on emotional states brought on by this recitative, just as in the preceding examples, the effect is quite different. Librettist and composer have built a scene in which a number of different emotions and a series of different musical ideas are welded together into a complex, flexible, yet coherent whole.

Some scenes such as the following one from the second act of Menotti's *The Consul* shift so repeatedly and quickly from recitative to aria to arioso and back to one type or another of recitative that it is difficult at first to see a relationship to a Metastasian recitative-aria structure. But the relationship is there: no matter how complex his construction, Menotti takes care to set as recitative all lines essential to an understanding of what is happening, all lines establishing an emotional state to be expanded by arioso or aria, all lines which he is particularly anxious for the audience to hear. It is impossible to understand every word of this scene without following the written text, just as it is impossible to understand every word of a Metastasian opera; but Menotti, by knowing exactly when to subordinate musical means to the text and when to allow his music to develop unrestricted by the libretto, has created a scene which, despite its highly complex structure and wide range of musical means, can be followed dramatically. The scene takes place in the consulate of an undesignated country; Magda Sorel has repeatedly tried to see the Consul to arrange to leave the country, but she has been able to get no further than the secretary's desk.

(ARIA):

MAGDA: To this we've come: that men withhold the world from
men.
No ship nor shore for him who drowns at sea.
No home nor grave for him who dies on land.
To this we've come:
that man be born a stranger upon God's earth,
that he be chosen without a chance for choice,
that he be hunted without the hope of refuge.
To this we've come, to this we've come;
and you, you too, shall weep.
If to men, not to God we now must pray,
tell me, Secretary, tell me, who are these men?
If to them, not to God, we now must pray,
tell me, Secretary, tell me.

(FREE, UNACCOMPANIED RECITATIVE):

Who are these dark archangels?
Will they be conquered? Will they be doomed?

(ARIA RESUMES):

Is there one—anyone behind those doors
to whom the heart can still be explained?
Is there one—anyone who still may care?
Tell me, Secretary, tell me.

(LIGHTLY ACCOMPANIED RECITATIVE):

Have *you* ever seen the Consul? Does he speak, does
he breathe?
Have *you* ever spoken to him?

(RECITATIVE, ACCOMPANIED BY CHORUS):

SECRETARY: I don't know what you're talking about! Of course you
can see the Consul . . . But he's a very busy man . . .
The appointment must be made in advance . . . You can
begin by filling this form and then I'll see what I can do
for you. Sign here. I said . . . sign here.

(ACCOMPANIED RECITATIVE):

MAGDA: Papers! Papers! Papers!

(FREE RECITATIVE):
But don't you understand?
What shall I tell you to make you understand?
(ACCOMPANIED RECITATIVE):
My child is dead . . . John's mother is dying . . . My
own life is in danger.
(FREE RECITATIVE):
I ask for help, and all you give me is . . . papers.
(ACCOMPANIED RECITATIVE):
What is your name? Magda Sorel. Age? Thirty-three.
Color of eyes? Color of hair? Single or married?
Religion and race? Place of birth, Father's name,
Mother's name?
Papers! Papers! Papers!
Papers, papers, papers!
Papers, papers, papers!
(ARIOSO):
Look at my eyes, they are afraid to sleep.
Look at my hands, at these old woman's hands.
(FREE RECITATIVE):
Why don't you say something? Aren't you secretaries
human beings like us? . . .
(ACCOMPANIED RECITATIVE):
What is your name? Magda Sorel. Age? Thirty-three.
(FREE RECITATIVE):
What will your papers do? They cannot stop the clock.
They are too thin an armor against a bullet.
(ACCOMPANIED RECITATIVE AND ARIOSO):
What is your name? Magda Sorel. Age? Thirty-three.
What does that matter? All that matters is that the time
is late, that I'm afraid and I need your help. What is your
name? What is your name? What is your name?
(ACCOMPANIED RECITATIVE):
This is my answer: My name—is woman. Age: still young.
Color of hair: Gray. Color of eyes: The color of tears.
Occupation: Waiting. Waiting. Waiting, waiting, waiting,
waiting, waiting.
(ARIA):
Oh! the day will come, I know,
        when our hearts aflame will burn your paper chains,
Warn the Consul, Secretary, warn him.
That day neither ink nor seal shall cage our souls.
That day will come, that day will come! [7]

[7] Copyright 1950 by G. Schirmer, Inc.

*George London as Boris Godunov, in the 1965 production by
The Opera Company of Boston.*

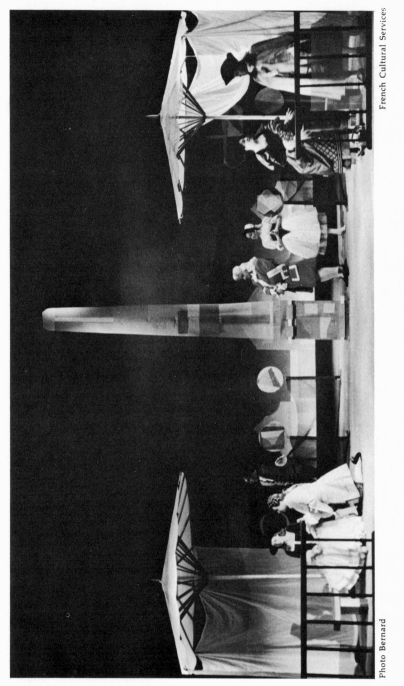

An ensemble scene from Mozart's opera buffa, La Finta Giardiniera, as produced in Paris.

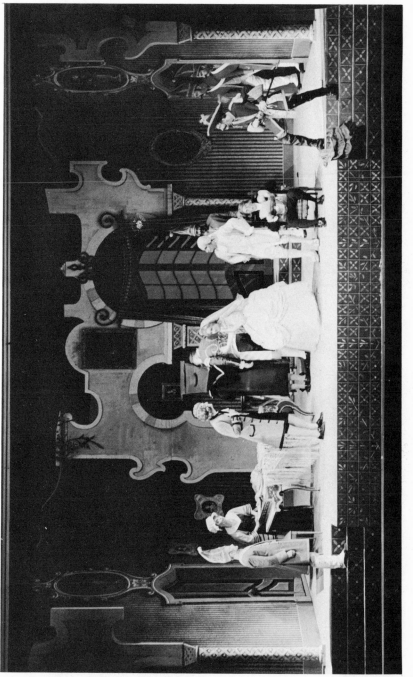

A scene from Rossini's The Barber of Seville, as done at Indiana University.

Menotti's Amahl and the Night Visitors, produced by NBC television.

This is a long way from Metastasio; the jaggedly irregular structure of the libretto, with abrupt shifts of mood, places it at the opposite end of the scale from Metastasio's controlled, balanced scenes. But the fundamental concept of recitative-aria function is still present.

🐚 SCENES IN RECITATIVE

Thus far recitative and aria have been considered together, and it has been shown how, when coupled, they can complement one another and form a scene with both musical and dramatic interest. The two may be used apart from one another, however, in certain situations.

Recitative which does not function as preparation for an aria is not at all uncommon in opera of a number of periods. A scene in which narration or dialogue essential to the dramatic development does not lead logically to a section of reflection or contemplation, or in which the librettist deliberately avoids the latter in order to move ahead to the next scene, will turn out musically as a scene of only recitative. The Metastasian libretti are sprinkled with such scenes, which contrast nicely with the more usual recitative-aria scenes.

The second act of Purcell's *Dido and Aeneas* ends with such a scene of recitative. The librettist thought of it as a climax in his drama—Aeneas is tricked into leaving Carthage, a decision which brings on the final tragedy—and he did not want to weaken the moment by introducing a totally unnecessary aria.

SPIRIT: Stay, Prince, and hear great Jove's command.
          He summons thee, this night, away.
AENEAS: Tonight?
SPIRIT: Tonight thou must forsake this land.
          The angry God will brook no longer stay. Jove commands
          thee, waste no more in Love's delights, those precious
          hours, allow'd by th' Almighty
          Pow'r to gain the Latian shore, and ruin'd Troy restore.
AENEAS: Jove's commands shall be obey'd,
          Tonight our anchors shall be weigh'd.
          But ah! what language can I try
          My injur'd Queen to pacify:
          No sooner she resigns her heart,
          But from her arms I'm forc'd to part.
          How can so hard a fate be took?

One night enjoy'd, the next forsook.
Yours be the blame, yet gods! For I obey your will, but
with more ease could die.

This is where the librettist wanted the act to end, on a dramatic
moment rather than a musical one. But it posed a problem for the
composer, for whom the idea of ending an act with the negligible
musical means of secco recitative was a disturbing one. He had no
choice but to set the scene as recitative, since the text must be
understood and since Aeneas' last ten lines shift so sharply in mood,
from obedience to sorrow to self-pity to angry defiance, that they
could not be set as a single aria. His solution was to set Aeneas' last
lines as *accompanied* recitative. The use of the orchestra gives the
scene more musical substance, and by writing a more expressive
melodic line than that normally found in recitative, one which includes
melismas and brief melodic flowerings, Purcell managed to preserve
and even intensify the dramatic effect of the scene, while at the same
time making it of more musical significance.

One of the most famous of all recitative scenes occurs in the
last act of Wagner's *Tannhäuser*. Tannhäuser has returned from a
pilgrimage to Rome, and in this scene he recounts incidents of his

journey, his brief audience with the Pope, the latter's refusal of his plea for pardon, and his resultant decision to resume his former life of lust and pleasure. None of this is known before Tannhäuser recounts it; the function of this portion of the libretto is purely narrative —a chain of events is recited, which must be heard and understood by the audience if they are to follow the progress of the drama.

TANNHAUSER: With fervor in my heart, as no other pilgrim
　　　　　Ever felt, I sought the way to Rome.
　　　　Ah, an angel had dispelled the pride of sin from my heart.
　　　　　　For her sake I went forth, a pilgrim,
　　　　　　　To seek salvation, which had been denied me;
　　　　　　　She who had pleaded for me with tears
　　　　　　　To seek to justify the tears she had shed
　　　　　　　For me, a sinner.
　　　　When on the road the most oppressed pilgrim walked
　　　　　near me;
　　　　It seemed as though my lot was too easy;
　　　　When his foot touched the soft ground of the meadows,
　　　　Then my foot sought thorns and stones;
　　　　When he his lips refreshed with cooling water,
　　　　Then did I shed my blood, to praise the Lord
　　　　I suffered in the hot rays of the sun;
　　　　When the wanderers were under shelter,
　　　　On ice and snow then I took rest at night;
　　　　So as not to see the wonders of fair Italy,
　　　　I closed my eyes while passing through its lands.
　　　　I did this, full of remorse,
　　　　To justify the tears of my angel.

　　　　Thus I arrived in Rome, and at the Holy place
　　　　I knelt in most fervent prayer;
　　　　Day broke—the bells were singing,
　　　　And heavenly songs resounded down;
　　　　Then all around I heard devout rejoicing—
　　　　Salvation to the multitude they promised.
　　　　Then I saw him, through whom God speaks.
　　　　The multitude knelt down in dust,
　　　　And grave he gave to thousands, made them free from sin.
　　　　He bid the thousands to rise.
　　　　Then I approached, with head bent down to earth,
　　　　With pitiful gestures I lamented,
　　　　Told of the lust that all my senses had felt,

And of the longing which could not be cooled;
I cried to him to relieve me
Of the hot fetters that yet did hold me.
And he, whom I thus begged, replied:

"If you have had such sinful lust,
And taken warmth from hellish fire,
If you have once been in Venus' mountain,
Then you are damned forever!
As this staff in my hand
Will never put forth leaves again,
So never can you be relieved
From the hot fire of hell! "

Then I sank down, crushed, my senses left me.
When I awoke, night had fallen on the deserted place.
In the distance I heard songs of grace.
Then I loathed the beautiful song,
From the deceitful sound of promise,
That cold as ice pierced through my soul,
Horror drove me off with steps so wild.
It drives me there, where I had once enjoyed
At her warm breast delightful pleasures!

To thee, fair Venus, I return,
Your beauty to enjoy again,
To thy court I will descend
And on thy breast forever rest.[8]

Dramatically, this is not recitative leading to an aria, but recitative complete in itself, planned as a central part of this act. Musically, the setting is mostly declamatory and syllabic, as recitative should be.

TANNHÄUSER

Da naht' auch ich   das Haupt ge-beugt zur Er - de, klagt' ich mich an

pp

poco cresc.

[8] Translation by Natalia Macfarren.

But in its utilization of the extreme range of the tenor voice,

its frequent abandonment of the stereotyped formulas of recitative in favor of a more expressive and melodic vocal line,

and its dramatic use of the full orchestra, this section is of far greater musical interest than most recitatives. Wagner has accomplished something difficult and rare in opera: this scene is both the musical and the dramatic climax of the act. It succeeds because of Wagner's genius in handling the materials of opera; but many later composers, attempting to write similar scenes, have fallen victim to the inherent danger of such a scene—if the musical means become too complex, the text will be lost, and there will be no dramatic effect whatsoever.

ARIA WITHOUT RECITATIVE

Composers rarely write arias without prefatory recitative, for reasons which should be clear from the preceding discussion of the function of recitative and aria. Arias occur only when dramatic situations have been clearly drawn; much of the text in most arias is obscured by the music, which assumes primary importance; and unless the audience knows the general emotional state of the character singing an aria, it may never learn it.

The third act of Gounod's *Faust* begins without recitative, however. The curtain opens on a single character, Siebel, who begins singing:

Gounod has set his text in syllabic fashion, with careful attention to proper accentuation, in the medium register of the mezzo voice, and has restricted his orchestra to very soft repeated chords which in no way interfere with the voice. This is more a song than an aria, and is labelled by the composer as such. There is nothing to prevent the text from being heard, and this text is simple, straightforward French which can be comprehended on first hearing. After a bit the song breaks into recitative, which again is in simple language and which clearly and directly sketches in the dramatic situation.

In general, if a composer decides to write an aria which is not preceded by recitative, he must restrict his musical means—particularly at the beginning—so as to allow his text to be heard. Thus the opening of the aria takes over the function of recitative, of setting the dramatic situation. Most arias found at the beginning of scenes are actually songs or cavatinas; another example is the Countess's cavatina *"Porgi amor"* opening the second act of Mozart's *The Marriage of Figaro*.

Occasionally an aria can be launched without preliminary recitative if the dramatic situation is clarified by other means: the set, the costume or deportment of the character or characters on stage, even pantomime. A number of recitativeless arias might be classified as "occupation arias;" a character appears on stage for the first time, from his dress we realize that he belongs to a certain profession, and he launches into a song or aria which has nothing to do with the development of the plot but rather furnishes local color or a pleasant musical interlude. In Mascagni's *Cavalleria Rusticana*, in the first act, we hear a jingling of bells and a cracking of whips offstage, then Alfio, a carter or waggoner, enters with some of his colleagues and sings a rousing song about the pleasures of his occupation, joined by a chorus of his friends. The entrance of Escamillo in Bizet's *Carmen* is strikingly similar: hailed in advance by a chorus, the bullfighter sings the famous "Toreador Song," in which he is joined by the chorus. Even Mozart has an "occupation aria;" in *The Magic Flute* Papageno strolls on, dressed in a suit of feathers and carrying a large bird cage and a pan-pipe, and without introducing himself in recitative sings of some of the details of his most peculiar line of work—but in a song, not an aria.

Aria without recitative must be handled carefully, in one of a certain number of limited ways, or the composer may find that he has lost his desired effect altogether.

✿ SUMMARY

The recitative-aria structure, a section of action leading to one of reflection in the libretto, is peculiar to opera and developed as the solution to the problem of balancing musical and dramatic interest. Some few operas do not use it, it may be treated in a flexible way, spoken dialogue may be substituted for recitative—but it is the most fundamental concept in opera, being used in some form almost from the first operas to the most recent ones.

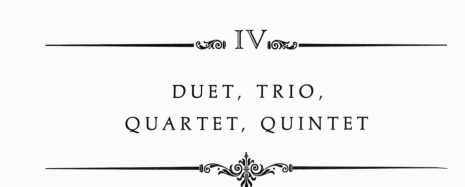

DUET, TRIO,
QUARTET, QUINTET

Although the arias in a setting of a Metastasian libretto had a satisfactory musical form, an entire act had none. It was made up of a string of recitative-aria scenes, relieved now and then by a scene in recitative and rarely a simple chorus, having no musical relationship to one another. They could be juggled around, transposed (in key), replaced, or eliminated at the will of the members of the cast. The composer's interest in musical structure went no further than the plan of the individual aria; the notion of organizing several scenes, or an entire act, into some larger formal musical structure was foreign to composers of the time. Opera as a large form was built on dramatic structure, not musical form.

We have seen in the previous chapter how some librettists (and composers) became concerned with the problem of organizing a more extended section of an opera into some coherent musical structure, and how they attacked the problem by building more extended and complex scenes which shifted freely and repeatedly from recitative of various sorts to arioso and aria. But the most fruitful approach to the problem of constructing scenes longer and more complex than Metastasian recitative-aria scenes, while retaining musical and dramatic coherence, has been to build them around two or more characters. A scene involving two singers (whether they sing consecutively or simultaneously) is called a *duet*, one with three singers a *trio*, four a *quartet*, five a *quintet*, six a *sextet*, seven a *septet*, and eight an *octet*.

Metastasio himself wrote duets on occasion. He would write a scene beginning in recitative, building up to some emotional state involving two of his characters, and climaxing with a poem identical in structure to an aria. The two characters would share the same text, which would be set by composers of the period as nothing more than an aria for two voices, with the two singers passing the same melodic material back and forth and probably singing together in parallel thirds or sixths at the end. The concept and structure of such a scene is in no way different from the usual recitative-aria pattern.

This is the simplest way to handle a scene involving two singers —to have it build through recitative to a point where they join in reflective music, singing the same (or similar) texts to the same musical material. Such a duet is built on a single emotion or dramatic situation, like a Metastasian aria, and suggests to the composer the same sorts of structures that he uses for his arias.

A scene of this sort occurs in the first act of Gounod's *Romeo and Juliet*, based on the famous Shakespearean drama. The opera begins at a masked ball; the first part of the first scene serving to set the mood and introduce several of the characters in the drama. The two principals are brought together alone for the first time in a brief scene of recitative.

ROMEO: The name of yonder charming maid? (*pointing to Juliet*)
GREGORIO: Do you not know? It is Gertrude.
GERTRUDE: (*turns around*) I beg your pardon?
GREGORIO: Pardon me, charming lady! They are calling for you below, supper is ready.
GERTRUDE: Indeed! I will go!
JULIET: Go! (*She leaves, with Gregorio. Juliet is about to follow.*)
ROMEO: I pray you, stay awhile.[1]

The two are left alone on the stage, and Romeo begins a simple song-like aria. The first lines are set simply and syllabically, so that the audience has no difficulty in understanding the text.

[1] Translation by Theodore Baker.

ROMEO

Ange a - do - ra - ble, Ma main cou - pa - ble

After a bit of this he pauses, and Juliet sings the same melodic material, with a different text but no change of mood.

JULIET

Cal - mez vos crain - tes! A ces é - trein - tes

Soon Juliet sings a different melodic phrase.

JULIET

Aux pri - è - res d'a - mour___ leur coeur reste in - sen - si - ble,

Romeo repeats this, with his own text.

ROMEO

E - xau-cez donc mes voeux___ et gar-dez im-pas-si-ble

And this tiny scene ends with the two singing together.

JUL.

Non! je l'ai pris!___ lais-sez-le moi! Non! je l'ai pris!___ lais-sez-le moi!

ROM.

Vous l'a-vez pris!___ ren-dez-le moi! Vous l'a-vez pris!___ ren-dez-le moi!

The effect of this duet is of unity. The two sing the same melodic lines; though the text gives some hint of the different personalities of the two, there is no attempt at musical characterization. One mood predominates, as in an aria, and there is no conflict, musically or dramatically.

A longer and more complex duet of this sort opens the third act of Donizetti's *Lucia di Lammermoor*. The curtain goes up on Edgar, seated alone in the castle of Ravenswood. A storm is raging outside, and a brief orchestral prelude depicts the rain, wind, and thunder. Edgar begins singing in simple recitative.

EDGAR: Dark is the night, and stormy, like my adverse fortune!

As he stands at the window, he sees someone approaching, heralded by galloping figures in the orchestra. Henry Ashton enters.

HENRY:	(throwing off his cloak) See me!
EDGAR:	What hath brought thee? Ashton?
HENRY:	Yes!
EDGAR:	Thou dar'st to brave me, whom thy treacherous arts have blighted?
HENRY:	I have come to avenge my honor.

Now follows a section which begins as an arioso for Edgar ("Here avenging shades surround thee, of thy victims, slain by treason"), but which breaks repeatedly into recitative. We learn that Henry has come to tell Edgar that his sister Lucia, whom Edgar loves, is to marry Sir Arthur Bucklaw. The bad blood between the two men boils, and Henry challenges Edgar to a duel.

EDGAR:	(with lofty disdain) We meet, then?
HENRY:	I'll meet thee when tomorrow's dawn begins to brighten.
EDGAR:	Where?
HENRY:	Near to the mould'ring tombs of Ravenswood.
EDGAR:	'Tis well. Yes, I'll meet thee there!
HENRY:	Soon shall that tomb close over thee.
EDGAR:	Boaster! There thou shalt die.

And the scene concludes with the two singing together, the same text to the same music.

EDGAR AND HENRY:

> Ah! The day of my vengeance no longer shall tarry,
> Nor swift retribution again shalt thou parry,
> The morning that dooms thee, the grave that entombs thee,
> No earthly resistance can longer avert.[2]

This is still a clearly recognizable recitative-aria scene. The first section often breaks into expressive recitative and even arioso, with musical interest momentarily intruding on the narration; the effect is not unlike that of the scene from *Madame Butterfly* discussed in the previous chapter, though the music is vastly different. Once the dramatic climax has been reached, the two characters, united in mood, sing the same music. It might well be called an *aria à due*.

Just as a recitative-aria structure can be expanded into a longer scene by alternation of several sections of recitative and aria, by

[2] Translation by Natalia Macfarren.

having the aria break into recitative and by free use of arioso during recitative, encompassing changes of mood and a series of musical ideas within a dramatic framework, so a duet can be made more complex. Many of the most successful operatic duets are built around two characters with different personalities, having different relationships to what has happened. They are brought together on the stage; a situation is developed in recitative which prompts one of them to launch into an aria or song; more recitative establishes a different situation, leading to another aria which probably contrasts in mood and musical material. Such alternation may continue, with new information brought out in recitative, arioso, or stage action prompting further contrasting music. The librettist often plans such a scene so that the two characters finally share a common emotional state; he can then give them the same—or similar—texts, and the composer may then have the two sing together to end the scene. With two characters to manipulate, two personalities to explore, the librettist finds it easier to construct a more extended scene. And once such a scene is sketched, the composer is able to use a variety of musical material, coherence being furnished by the dramatic structure of the libretto.

One of the most celebrated duets of this sort ends the first act of Puccini's *La Bohème*. Rodolfo, a young poet, sits alone in a garret he shares with his friends Schaunard, Marcel, and Colline. They have gone to the Latin Quarter, but he has decided to stay behind to work. There is a knock at the door, and Mimi appears with an extinguished candle to ask for a light. She is pale and soon faints; Rodolfo revives her, gives her some wine, lights her candle for her, and she prepares to leave. This is all sung in simple recitative, with stereotyped melodic figures, the orchestra occasionally giving out a fragment of a more melodic idea.

But Mimi has lost the key to her room. They drop to their knees and search for it on the floor; their candles go out, and they continue the search in the dark. Rodolfo finds the key, but puts it in his pocket without telling Mimi, and as they continue to grope for it, he takes her hand. This scene is set in arioso style: more attractive melodic ideas appear, and are repeated and passed back and forth between the two. This section (beginning with *"Oh! sventata, sventata!"*) is in a key (B♭) different from that of the recitative which precedes it (D), and uses completely different melodic material.

Holding Mimi's hand, Rodolfo sings an aria, telling of his life as a poet (*"Che gelida manina"*). The music moves to a new key (D♭, then A♭), the melodic material is new, and this is now in full-blown aria style, with more extended range for the singer and more elaborate use of the orchestra.[3]

Now it is Mimi's turn. Prompted by Rodolfo, she sings of her life as a seamstress ("*Si, Mi chiamano Mimi*" [3]): "Fine satin stuffs or silk I deftly embroider; so I am content and happy. The rose and lily I make for pastime. These flowers give me pleasure, as in magical accents they speak to me of love, of beauteous springtime. . . ." Again her music is in a new key (D), with new melodic material, unrelated

[3] Copyright 1897, 1917 by G. Ricordi & C.

musically to anything that has come before and quite satisfactory when taken by itself, apart from the music which surrounds it.

The voices of Rodolfo's friends are heard from outside, and he goes to the window to tell them to leave him alone a while longer. This is a brief interlude, in recitative.

Turning back to Mimi, he sings to her (*"O soave fanciulla"*), and the scene concludes with the two joining in a final duet section, declaring their love for one another. Once again the key is new (A, moving to C); the singers share the same melodic material, and for the first time in the entire prolonged duet, they sing together.[4]

This is a lengthy, complex scene, running through a rather wide gamut of emotions and a variety of musical ideas. It is built, musically and dramatically, as a chain of incidents.

		KEY
1.	preliminary recitative (from *"Non sono in vena"*)	D-G
2.	arioso à due (from *"Oh! sventata, sventata!"*)	B♭
3.	Rodolfo's aria (from *"Che gelida manina"*)	D♭
	(from *"In povertà mia lieta"*)	A♭
4.	Mimi's aria (from *"Si, Mi chiamano Mimi"*)	D
5.	recitative-interruption (from *"Ehi! Rodolfo!"*)	D
6.	final duet (from *"O soave fanciulla"*)	A
	recitative (from *"No, per pietà!"*)	A-C
	reprise (from *"Dammi il braccio"*)	C

Each of these sections is a unit itself. Dramatically, each is a small scene dealing with a single situation, with no conflict or contrast within it. Musically, each has its own tonal scheme and its own melodies. Several are often performed individually, detached from the large scene, and they make perfect sense alone. Thus, even though an extended scene has been built, it is merely a succession of clearly defined smaller scenes.

Another possibility is to bring together two characters who are somehow in conflict, and to have this conflict reflected in their text and in the music they sing. A brief but masterful example occurs in the second act of Mozart's *Don Giovanni*, with the licentious "hero" and the young peasant girl Zerlina as the principals. Zerlina is to marry Masetto. Don Giovanni has notions of his own, and in recitative he tries to persuade the young girl to come to his castle with him. She is confused, flattered to be the object of the attentions of a nobleman, but apprehensive about his intentions. The situation clearly drawn, the duet itself begins with the Don singing the principal melody, a sturdy 8-measure phrase beginning:

Zerlina replies, to the same music. Don Giovanni becomes more emphatic in his pleas, his mood reflected in the music by a bold, disjunct melodic line;

DON GIOVANNI

Vie - ni, mio bel di - let - to!

while Zerlina, still hesitant, has a melodic line which, with its chromaticism and slurred sixteenth notes, reflects her uncertain, nervous state.

ZERLINA

Pre - sto non son_ più_ for - te, non son più_ for - te, non son_ più_ for-te!

The principal melody now returns, but whereas before the Don had sung an entire phrase and come to a complete cadence before Zerlina began to sing, he now sings only two measures before she takes up the tune. She is still hesitant, but is being persuaded. The two are coming closer to an understanding, and Mozart shows this in his music by having the two voices almost overlap, then barely touch. Only such a great master of musical characterization as Mozart could write such attractive and appropriate music, and would go even beyond to underline the scene with this sort of symbolism.

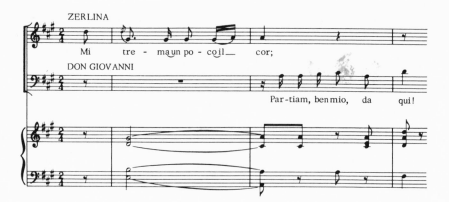

Now they sing together, but with the Don continuing his forceful, assertive line against Zerlina's wavering, hesitant melody. They are still in conflict, and the ear hears the differentiation of the two vocal lines.

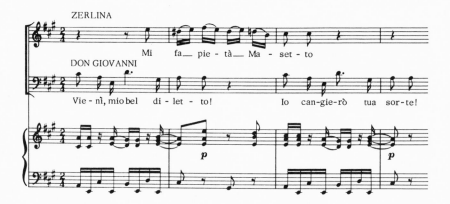

Two forceful commands by Don Giovanni (*"Andiam! Andiam!"*), and Zerlina yields. The conflict has been resolved, and with a change of meter and a new melodic idea, the two sing together (opposite).

Brief as this scene is, the librettist and composer have brought together two people in different emotional states and have managed to present these simultaneously. This is a different matter from having two people sharing the same emotion, as in the scenes from *Romeo and Juliet* and *Lucia di Lammermoor* discussed above, or from having them progress through consecutive moods, as in the scene from

La Bohème. This is one thing that opera can do more successfully than spoken drama.

LARGER ENSEMBLES

Librettists and composers building scenes around three or more singers use procedures similar to those just discussed for the duet. The "Card Trio" in the third act of Bizet's *Carmen* illustrates how three characters can be manipulated in a lengthy scene. Carmen sits brooding over her conversation with Don José in the recitative preceding this scene, a little apart from her friends Frasquita and Mercédès, who take out a deck of cards and begin telling fortunes. After some preliminary instructions to one another, in recitative, the two sing together to the cards, asking that they be truthful.

The game is in fun. In a second section they interpret the cards they turn up: Frasquita will be taken away to a mountain by a handsome young lover, who will turn out to be a chieftain, while Mercédès will marry a very old, very rich man who will make her a gift of a castle and then die, leaving her all of his riches.

Moderato FRASQUITA
f
Moi, je vois un jeune a-mou-reux, Qui m'aime on ne peut da-van-

ta - ge:

MERCÉDÈS
mf
Le mien est très riche et très vieux;

This first section of the trio is rounded off by a return to the music of the song to the cards, with the two singing together, as before.

Carmen now decides to see what the cards have to say to her. There is a change of mood and of key as she turns up cards and reads them, in recitative ("Diamonds! Spades! Death! They do not lie. First me, then him. For both of us—death!"). She continues to shuffle the cards and lay them out while singing a song completely different in musical material, mood, key, and every other respect from the music sung by Frasquita and Mercédès at the beginning of the scene.

The scene ends with the three singing together for the first time. The two friends resume their song to the cards, while Carmen sings fragments of her "song of fate" against them.

The structure of the scene, then, is:

Frasquita and Mercédès	preliminary recitative
	song to the cards (singing together)
	song of fortunes (singing consecutively)
	song to the cards (singing together)
Carmen	preliminary recitative
	song of fate
Frasquita, Mercédès, and Carmen	song to the cards, song of fate

The dramatic structure, which pits two of the characters against the third in sharply contrasting moods, is reflected in the music. What happens in the last section of the trio can happen only in opera: two completely different texts, set to different music, are presented simultaneously. Such an organization would not work in a spoken drama (or on television, or in the movies), since it would involve a dramatic absurdity. If two or more characters in a drama were to speak at the same time, it would be impossible for an audience to hear and comprehend what each was saying. They would be forced to listen to what one was saying and ignore the rest, or to simply give up and listen to nothing at all. Such a situation would be feasible only if it made no difference what was being said, or if the dramatic situation were so simple and so carefully prepared that the audience would know just what each of the actors was saying, whether or not they could hear them.

In the *Carmen* trio, Bizet offers several dramatic situations consecutively, and *only then* simultaneously. Two different texts are being sung at the end, at times—but these are the same texts which have already been heard. The three characters keep their same positions and poses on stage, and enough of the text can be heard for the audience to verify that it is indeed hearing again what it has already heard.

Verdi, another master of ensemble writing, succeeded—with the help of his librettist, Piave—in creating a memorable scene involving four characters, each in a completely different dramatic situation, in the third act of *Rigoletto*. The curtain goes up on a divided set, with a rustic inn occupying one half and the road which runs by it the other. Rigoletto and his daughter Gilda enter, come along the road to the inn, and stand outside looking in through a window; they can see the interior, but cannot be seen themselves from inside. In preliminary recitative we discover that Rigoletto has brought Gilda here to prove to her the unfaithfulness of her lover, the Duke of Mantua.

The Duke enters the inn, which is owned by the assassin Sparafucile, whose daughter Maddalena now comes down from the second floor. The Duke attempts to embrace her, but she is coy. While this skirmish is going on, Sparafucile slips outside, and in a brief whispered conversation with Rigoletto we are told that the latter has hired the assassin to kill the Duke later in the evening. Sparafucile leaves. At this point we know from what has been said, from the music, from the actions of the singers, and from the set, the exact emotional state of each of the singers. Rigoletto and Gilda form a pair on one side of the stage; he is vengeful, but elated that his plans to expose the Duke's infidelity and to have revenge for past insults are working so well, while his daughter is understandably anguished at seeing her lover enthusiastically pursuing another woman. The Duke and Maddalena form another pair inside, he embarked on a campaign of seduction, she (knowing of Rigoletto's plot) stalling him.

The quartet proper begins with the Duke singing to Maddalena.

DUKE: One day, if I remember rightly,
         Oh, beauty bright, I thee encountered,
         And ever since I've sought thee out,
         Till here at last I've found thee;
         Ah! now believe me while I swear,
         That henceforth this heart will thee adore.

Maddalena takes over.

MADDALENA: Ah, Ah! and since then twenty others
            Are by you quite as much remembered.
            (To give the gentleman his due, though,
            He has a cavalierlike bearing.)

While Gilda, watching through the window, can manage only a few interjections ("The villain! . . . Oh, father!") when the two inside pause at a cadence.

The Duke begins a second stanza of his song.

DUKE: What a beautiful, fair hand.

But this time he and Maddalena toss short phrases back and forth, Gilda and now Rigoletto have more interjections,

RIGOLETTO: Well! have you now heard enough?

and Verdi brings this section of the quartet to a rousing close by having the four sing together the lines they have just sung consecutively.

To this point Verdi has set his text so that most of it can be understood. Except for the Duke's opening lines, which are in the style of an aria, the setting has ranged from simple recitative to arioso, mostly syllabic, with a limited range. The text is not obscured by having two or more of the characters sing at the same time, except at the very end. The quartet is divided into two sharply contrasting sections, and this first one has somewhat the nature of a recitative.

But the second section is altogether different. The Duke begins a lyric passage, singing alone, but soon all four characters are singing completely different texts at the same time. Isolated words and an occasional phrase can be understood, but no more than this.

DUKE: Ah! of Venus the fairest daughter,
            The slave of your charms here behold;
            One word from thy beautiful lips
            My suffering alone can assuage;
            Come, and my fond heart relieve
            Of its anxious palpitations.

MADDALENA: Ah, ah! with all my heart I laugh
            At stories which so little cost;
            Your jokes I price, you may believe me
            At just as much as they are worth.
            Accustomed am I, my gallant signor,
            To badinage as good as this.

GILDA: Ah! thus to me of love he spoke,
            Thus the wretch hath me betrayed;
            Unhappy me! forlorn, deserted,
            With anguish how my heart doth ache!
            Oh! what a weak credulity
            In such a libertine to trust!

RIGOLETTO: Be silent; now to grieve is useless:
            That he deceived thee thus thou seest;
            Be silent, and on me depend
            Vengeance eternal to insure;
            Prompt as dreadful shall it be—
            Like thunder on his head 'twill fall! [5]

No harm is done by the fact that these words cannot be understood. The dramatic situation has become static, with the four characters merely repeating in other words what they have already said. Opera, which is forever fluctuating between the two polarities of drama and music, has here swung over almost completely to pure music. Almost—but not altogether. The scene can be performed as pure music, with the singers dropping their identities as characters in a drama, coming forward, facing the audience, and singing as though they were taking part in a recital. But Verdi has fashioned the scene so that even though almost all of the text is unintelligible, something in the music still sets off the four different personalities. The four singers do not share the same melodic material; each has his own vocal line, reflective of the emotional state of the character he is portraying. The Duke attempts to charm Maddalena with a suave, lyric melodic line.

[5] Translation by Geo. W. Tryon, Jr.

DUCA

Fi -glia del -l'a- mo - re, schia-vo son de' vez-zi tuo - i;

Maddalena sings quick, staccato passages suggestive of her coy but flirtatious state.

MADDALENA

Ah! Ah! ri-do ben di co-re, chè tai ba-ie co-stan po-co;

quan-to val-ga il vo -sto gio-co, mel, cre-de - te, so ap-prez- zar.

Gilda's anguish comes out in chromatic sliding notes, expressive appoggiaturas, syncopated throbbing repeated tones, and desperate high notes.

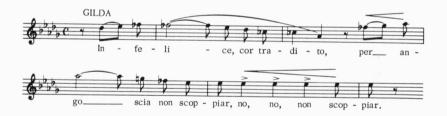

GILDA

In - fe - li - ce, cor tra - di - to, per___ an -

go_____ scia non scop - piar, no, no, non scop - piar.

Rigoletto, in control of the situation and confident of revenge, sings solid diatonic passages, with many repeated notes, in a strongly declamatory style.

RIGOLETTO

Ta-ci e mia sa - rà la cu - ra la ven-det-ta d'af-fret - tar.

At no point is there exchange of melodic material. If the four singers hold their position on stage and keep the proper pose, the effect is of four contrasting things taking place simultaneously. The quartet works, then, for two reasons: the dramatic situation of each of the four characters has been clearly sketched in text, action, and music, before the most elaborate musical means are used; and Verdi has carefully given each of them characteristic melodic material.

A distinction must be made between this type of dramatic ensemble and the sort found in the first act of Beethoven's *Fidelio*. Florestan, a Spanish nobleman, has been imprisoned for political reasons by the evil Pizarro. His wife Leonora, hoping to rescue him, has disguised herself as a young man named Fidelio and found employment at the prison where she suspects her husband is held. The jailer, Rocco, has a daughter, Marcellina, who is attracted to "Fidelio," to the dismay of her former sweetheart, Jaquino. The four—Leonora, Rocco, Marcellina, and Jaquino—are brought together in the fourth scene, and in a section of spoken dialogue (since this is a Singspiel) Rocco lets it be known that he thinks highly of his new helper Fidelio, that he knows of his daughter's infatuation with the young "man," and that he would look with favor on a match between the two. Marcellina looks affectionately at Fidelio and the quartet begins.

MARCELLINA: Within this heart I hide
The love I feel for thee;
If I may be thy bride
How happy shall I be!

LEONORA: Alas, which way shall I
From this new danger fly?
She loves me, I can see;
But all her love is pain to me!

ROCCO: She loves him, it is clear,
Yes, yes, my daughter dear!
Thy wishes I can see;
And Fidelio shall thy husband be.

JAQUINO: Ah! me, what do I hear?
No hope for me, I fear!
My senses go astray,
I know not what to say.[6]

Musically, the quartet is imitative, with each of the four singers having the same melodic material in turn. Marcellina sings her four

[6] Translation by Percy Pinkerton.

An ensemble scene from Mozart's Così fan Tutte, as produced by the University of Illinois Opera Workshop.

lines of text alone (accompanied by the orchestra); when Leonora begins, Marcellina continues, singing her text again in counterpoint against the main melody presented by Leonora. Rocco's entrance is sung against both of the women, and when Jaquino sings his strophe, all four texts are going on simultaneously. The audience has no difficulty in following Marcellina's text, but with each succeeding entrance, comprehension of the text becomes more difficult because of the accumulation of voices singing different sets of words. But it is unnecessary for all of the text to be understood. With the four singers sharing the identical melody, there is no musical differentiation among them, and the effect is of unity, not of conflict or contrast. Dramatically, a static point has been reached, with all four characters now aware of Marcellina's love for Leonora. A reading of the libretto reveals that the texts sung by the four reflect their different attitudes toward this development, but this does not come across in a performance of the opera because of the obscuring of much of the text and the similarity of musical material. This is just as Beethoven planned matters, of course. The libretto is fashioned so that this part of the text is dispensable. Nothing essential to the unfolding of the plot is presented, no lines give new insight into the personalities of the characters. Here, much more so than in the *Rigoletto* quartet, the interest has become almost purely musical.

Certain critics and historians of opera seem to have had a curious misconception about such ensemble scenes, imagining that it is possible for a number of characters to sing different texts simultaneously, for all of these texts to be comprehended by an audience, and for a dramatic effect to be created thereby.

One of the loveliest trios in all opera occurs shortly before the end of Strauss's *Der Rosenkavalier*. The three main protagonists have been brought together on the stage: the Marschallin, whose love affair with the young nobleman Octavian has ended; Octavian himself (sung by a mezzo-soprano); and the young Sophia, more his own age, with whom he is now in love. The dramatic climax of the opera has been reached, with the Marschallin recognizing that the two are in love and giving them her blessings, and the three meditate on the situation in the trio.

MARSCHALLIN:

> I made a vow to love him rightly, as a good woman should.
> E'en to love the love he bore another I promised . . .
> But in truth I did not think that all so soon the task would await me.

For many a thing is ordained in this world
Which we should scarcely believe could be,
    If we heard others tell of them;
But some day whom they wound believes in them, and
    knows not how.
There stands the boy, and here stand I,
    And with his love, new-found this day, he will have
        happiness,
Such as a man thinks the best the world can give.
    So be it.

SOPHIA: I feel as one at worship, holiest thoughts fill my soul;
And yet by most unholy thought and sinful I'm possessed.
With holiest thoughts my soul is filled.
At yonder lay's feet I fain would kneel, yet fain would I
    harm her;
For I feel she gives him to me and yet robs me of part of
    him.
So strangely I'm distraught.
All things would I know, yet fear to know the truth.
Now longing to ask, now fearing; hot am I and cold.
(to Octavian) And know but you, know but one thing, that
    I love you.

OCTAVIAN: What thing so wond'rous has come to pass?
I fain would ask her; Can it be?
And just that question that I know I cannot ask of her.
I fain would ask her: Oh why trembles my soul?
Has a great wrong, a foul deed been done?
And just of her I may not ask the question.
(to Sophia) And then on your dear face I gaze, and see but
    you,
Know but you, Sophia, and see but you, and nothing know
    but this:
You are the one I love.[7]

After the Marschallin's first line, which she sings alone, the
three sing together until her last line, which is likewise delivered
alone. In between these two lines, almost nothing of the text is
comprehensible to an audience. Though the three are in somewhat
different emotional states, the voices weave together with the orchestra as parts of a single musical mood. The three texts are reflective,
and the effect is of three aria texts being sung simultaneously. In

reading through the libretto, it is difficult to escape the impression that these lines represent the culmination of the drama. Certainly the librettist lavished care on these texts, which are far removed from the hack poetry which too often serves for aria texts.

This trio contains excellent music, and excellent poetry. But it is a mistake to pretend that the two are enjoyed together in a performance of this scene. The music wins out completely, and the poetry can be enjoyed only from a reading of the libretto.

Similar scenes are the quintet at the end of the third act of Wagner's *Die Meistersinger* and the quintet near the end of the last act of Samuel Barber's *Vanessa.* In each, a static point has been reached in the drama; in each, the five singers have different texts which make interesting reading but which are never heard in the opera house for the very good reason that when five different texts are sung simultaneously, nothing of any one of them can be heard. Both quintets are musical peaks of the act in which they occur. Neither is dramatic.

SUMMARY

Ensemble scenes involving two or more of the principal singers may be constructed in a number of ways. Many of them are nothing more than simple recitative-aria scenes, with the musical material of the aria shared by the singers involved. Other are similar in structure to more elaborate recitative-aria scenes, with freer alternation between various sorts of recitative, arioso, and aria. In another common and effective type of ensemble scene, the singers alternate in aria-like sections, each perhaps introduced by a bit of recitative and contrasting in mood and melodic material, then sing a final section together.

Finally, some of the more skillful operatic composers have been able to build ensemble scenes in which two or more singers, in different emotional states, are given individual melodic material. The result is that contrasting or conflicting moods are presented at the same time. Such a scene has no parallel in spoken drama.

V

FINALE AND INTRODUCTION

Though ensembles may occur at any point in an opera, composers of the last several centuries have been particularly fond of using them as act endings. They like the effect of collecting a number of the principal singers on stage and involving them in a complex scene, musically and perhaps dramatically, to bring the act to an impressive close.

Historically, this was the first type of ensemble to be developed. The simple comic operas of the eighteenth century, those of Pergolesi and his contemporaries in other countries, were built of a series of recitative (or spoken dialogue) and aria scenes, but the last act ended with all of the main characters brought together for the final scene, a duet for a two-character opera, a trio for one with three main singers.

The term *finale* is used for such a scene, which may be similar in structure to the types of ensembles discussed in the previous chapter, but which in the hands of certain composers may become even more complex and involve more musical and dramatic elements than would be found in an ensemble scene occurring at another place in the act.

Donizetti's *L'Elisir d'Amore,* a comic opera, ends with a quite simple finale. All complexities of the plot have been resolved, the dramatic climax has been reached (the two lovers, Adina and Nemorino, have been brought together, to the dismay of the "villain" Belcore), and Dulcamara, the itinerant doctor whose "love potion" has figured so prominently in the drama, is leaving to peddle his wares in another village. Dulcamara sings a stanza of a simple song.

54387

The finale of the last act of Puccini's The Girl of the Golden West. The Metropolitan Opera production of 1910, with Enrico Caruso and Emmy Destinn, in the center, in the leading roles.

DULCAMARA: My elixir is perfection, it's the pride of my profession,
And it is the prize possession of my fabulous collection;
It will pacify your babies, cure the measles and the rabies,
Clear complexions when they mottle or what else the case
may be.[1]

A chorus of villagers, assembled for the climax of the drama,
sings at the end of this stanza ("Doctor, please I want a bottle!
Give me one, here two, here three!"), then Dulcamara sings another

[1] Translation by Ruth and Thomas Martin. Copyright 1960, 1961 by G.
Schirmer, Inc.

stanza of his song to exactly the same music ("It's a treat for zealous tutors who give lessons in your houses . . ."). The villagers sing again when he pauses for breath, then the doctor launches a third stanza ("It is written in the heavens that I leave you this great treasure . . ."), this time with the villagers joining in shortly before he completes his words.

From this point to the end, the entire cast joins in a general uproar. The villagers hail the doctor ("Here's to Doctor Dulcamara, may he always be our friend!"), the two lovers thank him for his aid ("I owe all to Dulcamara; if I live to be a hundred, I'll be grateful to the end."), Belcore expresses his anger at being foiled ("You're a quack and you have blundered! I will hate him to the end! You never were my friend!"), and Dulcamara shouts his good-bys. Needless to say, none of this text can be understood—but there is no reason for it to be. (See page 93.)

This finale is a single dramatic and musical unit. The situation is static, with each singer merely repeating ideas which he has already stated. The music is in one key throughout, organized around the stanzas of the doctor's song. It is nothing more than a brief reflective quartet, with supporting chorus, no more complex in structure than the most simple ensemble scene which might occur anywhere in an act.

Most finales are more complex than this, however, since composers often find it desirable to bring acts to a brilliant close which will give a feeling of climax by overshadowing all that has come before. The finale to the first act of Bellini's *Norma* is the lengthiest section to this point in the opera, the most elaborate structurally, and at the end draws on more musical resources than have been used before in the work. It begins with accompanied recitative between Norma, a Druid high priestess, and Adalgisa, a younger priestess.

Norma has borne two children to Pollione, the Roman proconsul. Adalgisa herself has been involved with a Roman. Norma questions her to find out his identity, and Pollione, entering at this point, is identified by Adalgisa as her lover. This news throws Norma into a rage—and a florid arioso.

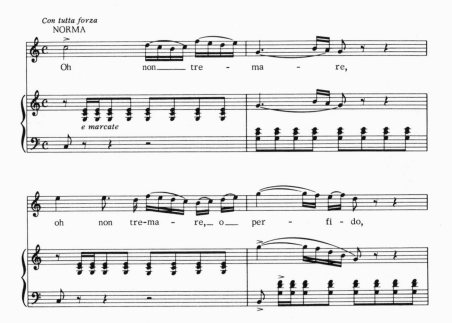

Now a few measures of recitative lead to a change of key and meter, and to a trio in which the three offer their views on this awkward situation, first one after another, then all together.

NORMA: Oh, now the traitor thou dost know,
Who basely would betray thee,
Better thou wert in death laid low,
Than that his falsehood, his deceit should sway thee.

POLLIONE: Norma! thy wrathful soul I know,
Spare me thy stern upbraiding,
Unto this maid some pity show,
Ah, see what fears her heart invading.

ADALGISA: Oh day of endless bitter woe!
While I their fatal secret know,
I dread to listen or to gainsay them,
Oh, would on earth we ne'er had met! [2]

More dramatic recitative leads to a brief arioso by Pollione, with interjections by the two angry women.

Another change of key and meter brings a florid trio. Norma insists that Pollione leave, and swears to have revenge on him; Adalgisa and Pollione sing together, begging her to relent; then all three sing together, first in unison and then alternately.

Finally a sacred shield is struck and an offstage chorus summons Norma to the temple. The three principals sing against this chorus, Norma urging the other two to leave, Pollione insisting that he still loves her and will stay. This mass of sound gives an impressive musical ending to the act (opposite).

This finale, then, is built of a series of episodes; a type of structure we have already seen in ensemble scenes. Each episode has its own musical material, often with its own key and meter.

[2] Translation by Natalia Macfarren.

		KEY	METER
1.	Accompanied recitative: Norma, Adalgisa, Pollione	C major	4/4
2.	Florid arioso: Norma	C major	4/4
3.	Trio: Norma, Adalgisa, Pollione	Bb major	9/8
4.	Accompanied recitative—dramatic arioso: Pollione	Eb major	4/4
5.	Trio: Norma, Adalgisa, Pollione	g minor	4/4
6.	Trio with five-part chorus	G major	4/4

This finale is constructed so that the audience can sit back and enjoy the music without having to worry about intricacies of plot. The only dramatic point of significance is the identification of Pollione as Adalgisa's lover, which leads to the fury of the two women. This point is made in recitative, underlined by stage action. The emotional states of the three, following this revelation, are so predictable and so stereotyped that they can be sketched in with a few broad operatic gestures, and the audience can devote its full attention to the singing, which is the main point of this section of the opera anyway.

Mozart was perhaps the greatest master of the finale in the entire history of opera, and an examination of such a finale as that of the second act of *The Marriage of Figaro* will reveal how a composer of genius, working with a first-rate librettist, can transform an ensemble scene into something quite different from any we have examined thus far. The first striking thing about this finale is its length: it occupies more pages of score and takes more time in performance than all the rest of the numbers in the act put together. Many finales are built around a certain number of the principals who are on stage for the entire ensemble, perhaps supported by a chorus; but in this one, characters come and go, and various sections of the finale are for different groups of singers. Many composers and librettists fashion finales around static dramatic points, to allow the music to become as involved as the composer may wish; in *Figaro*, each section of the finale moves the drama to another point until finally the dramatic high point of the act is reached—but never at the expense of musical interest. The finale can best be described by discussing each of its smaller sections in turn.

1. Duet: Count, Countess. The Count believes that he has trapped a young page, Cherubino, in a closet in the Countess's room. The Countess pleads that the young boy is innocent, and begs her husband to be gentle with him: the Count approaches the closet door with drawn sword, accusing his wife of shameful behavior and swearing vengeance on Cherubino.

2a. Trio: Susanna, Count, Countess. Unknown to the Countess, Cherubino has jumped out of a window and Susanna has taken his place in the closet. When the Count throws open the door, Susanna steps out and greets them, while they both express their astonishment at finding her there.

2b. Trio: the above. After a few preliminary recitative-like phrases, the tables are turned: the Count begs forgiveness for his suspicions and accusations, and Susanna and the Countess berate him for having so little faith in his wife. The three sing alone, in pairs, and finally all together.

3a. Quartet: Figaro, Count, Susanna, Countess. Figaro enters, telling them that it is time for his wedding with Susanna to begin. The Count insists on questioning him for a moment first, and the two ladies whisper to Figaro to be on his guard.

3b. Quartet: the above. The Count shows Figaro a letter, asking him if he has seen it before. The latter says he has not, though the ladies warn him that they have told the Count about the plot involving the letter. Figaro brushes this off and insists that the Count give his blessings to the marriage. The latter delays, since he has plans for Susanna himself and has his own plot underway—to prevent the marriage.

4. Quintet: Antonio, Count, Susanna, Countess, Figaro. Antonio, the gardener, rushes in to report that he has seen someone jump from the window of the Countess's room into some of his flowers. The Count's suspicions are rekindled, but Figaro, prompted by Susanna and the Countess, says that it was he, and hobbles around to show that his ankle was hurt in the jump.

5. Quintet—Quartet: the above. Antonio gives the Count a paper which he says was dropped by the person whom he saw leap from the window, then leaves. The Count taunts Figaro, asking him to identify the document. Again prompted by the women, he says that it is Cherubino's commission, which he was taking to be sealed.

6a. Septet: Marcellina, Basilio, Bartolo, Count, Countess, Susanna, Figaro. The Count's confederates enter, and his plot is revealed: Marcellina, a housekeeper, claims to have a contract signed by Figaro in which he promises to marry *her*.

6b. Septet: the above. Grouped three (Susanna, Countess, Figaro) against four (Marcellina, Basilio, Bartolo, Count), the characters comment on this new turn of events. No new dramatic material is introduced, and the ending is purely and impressively musical, with all seven singing together against full orchestra.

		KEY	METER
1.	Duet: Count, Countess ("*Esciomai, garzon malnato*")	E♭ major	$\frac{4}{4}$, *allegro*

2a. Trio: Susanna, Count, Countess ("*Signore! Cos'è quel stupore*")	B♭ major	$\frac{3}{8}$, *molto andante*
2b. Trio: the above ("*Susanna, I morta*")	B♭ major	$\frac{4}{4}$, *allegro*
3a. Quartet: Figaro, Count, Susanna, Countess ("*Signore, di fuori*")	G major	$\frac{3}{8}$, *allegro*
3b. Quartet: the above ("*Conoscete, Signor Figaro*")	C major	$\frac{2}{4}$, *andante*
4. Quintet: Antonio, Count, Susanna, Countess, Figaro ("*Ah! Signor*")	F major	$\frac{4}{4}$, *allegro molto*
5. Quintet—Quartet: the above ("*Vostre dunque saran queste carte*")	B♭ major	$\frac{6}{8}$, *andante*
6a. Septet: Marcellina, Basilio, Bartolo, Count, Countess, Susanna, Figaro ("*Voi signor, che giusto siete*")	E♭ major	$\frac{4}{4}$, *allegro assai*
6b. Septet: the above (*Son confuso, son stordito*")	E♭ major	$\frac{4}{4}$, *più allegro— prestissimo*

Mozart and Da Ponte introduce a series of important new dramatic points in the course of this finale. Interestingly, this is done without resort to recitative. Mozart carefully sets those lines containing information essential to the development of the drama in a syllabic fashion, in medium range, against light orchestration. Admittedly the situations are rather broad, and are clarified by the positioning of the characters on stage, by gestures, pantomime, and by the music itself. Nevertheless, the fact remains that librettist and composer have brought about and developed changing dramatic situations without using recitative.

Except in the finales, this opera is built of the usual recitative-aria and recitative-ensemble scenes. But in this finale Mozart demonstrates that there is another way of putting an opera together.

Ensemble scenes serving as act beginnings are called *introductions*. This term has a specific meaning: it is not used for any sort of first scene, but for one involving some of the principal singers and often a chorus. Its function is similar to that of the finale—to begin an act with an impressive musical section of some duration involving large musical forces—and its structure is usually also similar to one of the types of finales.

The first act of Rossini's *Count Ory* begins with such a scene. The curtain goes up on a group of villagers collecting around Raimbaud, who makes it clear from his gestures that he has something to tell them.

RAIMBAUD: Ladies, come quickly to listen to the wise hermit;
            He will stop here on the way to the hermitage.
            Let us give him our offerings and our prayers, as he passes.

Alice sings with a six-part chorus of the villagers ("Here's a question: will he have a good suggestion how to win and hold a mate?"), and the scene continues as a dialogue between Raimbaud and Alice, who is always supported by the chorus. A banquet is prepared, wine is brought, and this section of the introduction concludes with everyone singing together.

Ragonde enters from the castle, the music becomes quieter and modulates, and this new character begins singing in arioso style:

RAGONDE: As the countess is, alas, unhappy,
           Why should such merry songs be sung by her subjects?
           When one loves his mistress, he takes her sadness to heart.
           She wishes to visit with the good hermit,
           In hopes that he may deliver her from her troubles.

She explains that the countess has decided to summon the Count Ory, who has a reputation for being able to cure anything, in the hope that he can bring her out of her depressed state. Since it was the Count whom the villagers, and Alice and Raimbaud, were preparing to receive, the music returns to its original key and mood, and the introduction ends with the three principals and the chorus joining forces.

This introduction, then, is an ensemble scene in two sections, the first a duet with chorus, the second a trio with chorus.

Introductions and finales may differ from ensembles occurring elsewhere in a scene in their use of chorus along with principal singers, and in their frequently more flexible structure, with characters coming and going and different sections consequently involving different numbers of singers. As we saw with the finale to the second act of Mozart's *The Marriage of Figaro*, the finale may grow to such a size that it will dwarf what has come before, and may contain both the musical and the dramatic climax of the act; the introduction occasionally takes on similar dimensions.

For example, the first act of Rossini's *William Tell* is made up of seven extended but clearly defined sections: an introduction; a recitative and duet; a recitative and chorus; another recitative and chorus; a section of dance ("*Passo à sei*"); another dance, with chorus; and a finale. The introduction is 640 measures in length and the finale 560; the 1200 measures of these two combined are almost as much as the 1300 measures taken up by the entire remainder of the act. These two sections almost overwhelm what comes in between by sheer volume of sound as well. The introduction progresses through various combinations of voices to a final section in which six of the principals sing with a six-part chorus, and the finale closes with five soloists, a soldier's chorus (male voices), and a seven-part chorus of Swiss citizens. And Meyerbeer's *L'Africaine* has a first act made up only of a recitative section leading to a "Romance" by Inez (soprano); another scene of recitative leading to a trio by Inez, Don Pedro, and the Admiral; and then the finale, involving five singers and a male chorus, which is more than three times as long as the rest of the act.

In finales (and to a lesser extent in introductions), composers and librettists have explored methods of building longer, more complex sections of continuous, coherent music than has been possible in recitative-aria or even recitative-ensemble scenes. In some operas, the finale (and perhaps the introduction) are allowed to grow to such a size that their organization pervades quite long stretches. Eventually, as we will see in a later chapter, the method of organization found in the finale replaced the traditional recitative-aria method for entire acts, and even entire operas.

✿ SUMMARY

A finale is an ensemble scene occurring at the end of an act; an introduction is one opening an act. They may resemble other ensembles in structure: they may be static dramatically, with all of the characters involved joined in music reflective of one situation; or they may be built as a chain of episodes, with contrasting musical material. But some finales are built in another way, with changing dramatic situations and much more flexible musical structures. The finale may be of a size comparable to the previous sections of an act, but it may also overwhelm what has come before, in length and musical forces.

VI

THE CHORUS

None of the basic elements of opera has been treated in as variable a fashion as the chorus. At certain periods in the history of opera, composers and audiences have been interested primarily in the vocal and dramatic performance of individual singers, the "stars;" many operas make no use whatsoever of a chorus, or have it perform some perfunctory task as a relief from the main business of the opera. At the other end of the scale we have operas in which the chorus plays a prominent part in the dramatic and musical development of the work, may have as much to do as any of the principals, and may be of an impressive size. The composer may perhaps call for a double or even triple chorus.

There is sometimes variation according to the type of opera. At times, comic opera has tended to use less chorus than serious opera; the chorus was absolutely indispensable in the so-called "grand opera" of the nineteenth century; and we rarely find a chorus in the "chamber opera" of this century. Sometimes composers of one nationality are more fond of the chorus than are those of another. More to the point for our purposes, composers of various nationalities, throughout the history of opera, have found a rich variety of uses for the chorus. The solo performers in opera keep their identities as characters in a drama, whether they are singing alone or in ensemble. At any given moment they are either presenting new information to move the drama forward, or are involved in reflection on what has happened. As we shall see, the chorus may do either of these two, also—but it may function in a number of other ways. In the hands of an imaginative composer and librettist, the chorus may serve a multiplicity of purposes.

THE CHORUS AS SCENERY

In many operas, the first curtain of an act opens on a chorus already on stage, or in the process of assembling. The members are dressed as villagers or soldiers or peasants or students or townspeople, and carry the tools of whatever trade they represent. They stand around in groups or circulate about the stage, greeting one another, slapping friends on the back, and pretending to engage one another in small personal conversations. They sing about the weather, or the season, or their profession, or about the joys or sorrows of living wherever they are supposed to live. This goes on for awhile, until finally the opera gets down to more serious business with the entrance of one or more of the principals. For the audience—and usually for the director—this has all been preliminary matter, a few minutes of diversion before the opera proper begins. The chorus has performed the function of setting the stage for the first scene, of helping to establish the locale, or of setting the mood prevailing as the act begins. The text they sing has no significance in the development of the drama.

A chorus used this way is performing exactly the same function as the sets and the lighting. It helps sketch a visual background, against which action is to take place. It is nothing more than part of the scenery.

A typical chorus of this sort opens Smetana's *The Bartered Bride*. The set depicts a village in Bohemia, with an inn to one side. Peasants are gathered on stage, and they launch into a chorus about the joys of the spring season.

> Now is the time ripe for mating,
> Maypoles all are decked and waiting,
> Weave a garland round about, the while we sing,
> Weave a garland in and out, round a ring.
> All the world is drunk with this delicious spring![1]

After a bit of this, the opera settles down to business.

Mascagni's *Cavalleria Rusticana* begins with a quite similar scene. This time the village is in Sicily, and a church replaces the inn, but

[1] Translation by Marian Farquhar. Copyright 1956 by G. Schirmer, Inc.

104   THE CHORUS

everything else is the same. Peasants—men, women, and children—cross the square and enter the church, as bells toll. Women's voices are heard, offstage.

> Blossoms of orange sweeten the vernal air,
> Carol gay larks 'mid the myrtles in flow'r. . . .

The women enter, singing, and we see that they are peasants. Now male voices are heard from the distance.

> 'Mid fields of golden corn, across the meadows,
> We hear your spinning wheels and merry voices. . . .

The men enter, and the scene is brought to a conclusion by having everyone on stage join forces as the men and women sing together. All leave, and the stage is empty again. Nothing of dramatic importance has happened. The people who have been on stage play no part in the drama which will soon unfold, and they have sung nothing which has any bearing on later events. They, and the set, have told us only that the action will take place in a Sicilian village on an Easter Sunday morning. It should be noted that this opera turns out to be a tragedy, while *The Bartered Bride* is a comedy throughout, yet they begin with comparable scenes using quite similar musical ideas. Since such opening chorus scenes are so disassociated from the drama to follow, the librettist and composer make no attempt to have them match its mood.

Two more familiar operas which begin in similar fashion will be cited. Offenbach's *Tales of Hoffman* opens in a tavern, with students entering and shouting for wine and beer. After they have been served they call for Hoffman, the poet, to entertain them with stories of his adventures, and it is against this backdrop that he tells the three fantastic tales that form the three acts of the opera. The first curtain in Wagner's *Die Meistersinger* goes up on the interior of St. Catherine in Nuremberg, with the congregation singing a chorale, against which Eva and Walther enact a pantomime. The text of the chorale has nothing to do with what happens, of course, but is merely part of the scenery of the opening section of the opera.

The scenery in an opera may be an attractive picture against which the action is to be played, setting the locale and time of the drama. But it may also establish a mood. The audience can often tell, with the first curtain, whether a gay comedy or a somber tragedy will unfold, merely from the effect created by the sets and lighting. For example, the second tableau of the third act of Massenet's *Thaïs* takes place on the banks of the Nile, in the village of the Cenobites. The set should represent such a village as accurately as possible. But there is also a stage direction to the effect that a storm is approaching. Stormy unsettled emotions will be depicted during this scene, and the librettist asks that the stage picture prepare the audience for them. The lighting should be dim, with a sinister crimson in the sky in the west and occasional flashes of lightning. And since the chorus is used here as part of the stage picture, their words reinforce the mood.

CENOBITES: Heavy clouds fill the sky!
What oppressive air weighs down ev'rything about us!
One can hear afar the cry of the jackal!
The wind will soon unchain its roaring pack of bloodhounds,
With the aid of lightning and thunder! [2]

An effective refinement in the use of the chorus to establish a mood occurs in Leonard Bernstein's short opera *Trouble in Tahiti*. A trio, "a Greek Chorus born of the radio commercial," sketches a backdrop of what appears to be a happy American household, a suburban family with everything that most Americans seem to want: an expensive home, money, a family, security.

TRIO: Mornin' sun kisses the windows: kisses the walls
Of the little white house;
Kisses the doorknob: kisses the roof,
Of the little white house in Scarsdale.
Friendly sun opens the eyelids: opens the eyes
Of the husband and wife;
Kindles their faces: kindles their love
In the little white house in Scarsdale
Suburbia! Our little spot, out of the hubbub,
Less than an hour by train.
Suburbia! Sweet in the spring, healthful in winter,
Saves us the bother of summers in Maine.

But when the first scene begins, with the husband and wife at the breakfast table, we immediately see that their life is not so idyllic after all.

SAM: How could you say
The thing that you did . . .

[2] Translation by Hermann Klein.

DINAH:	What is it this time?
SAM:	In front of the kid!
DINAH:	You were the first To go up in smoke.
SAM:	Always it's *my* fault!
DINAH:	I just meant a joke.
SAM:	Pass me the toast.
DINAH:	You might have said please.[3]

And throughout the opera we follow Sam and Dinah through a typical day of quarrels and frustrations, played against the recurring chorus which continues to paint a cheerful glowing picture of the attractive external features of their life.

A curiously similar scene, in which a chorus paints one mood against a violently contrasting scene played out by the principals, occurs at the very end of Massenet's *Werther*. The young Werther, finally convinced that his passion for Charlotte is futile, has shot himself and lies mortally wounded at his table. Charlotte enters.

CHARLOTTE:	Werther! Werther! God! Oh! There's blood! No! No! This cannot be! He's not dead! O Werther!

He is not dead, of course: there is just enough life left in him to sing the final duet.

WERTHER:	Ah, Charlotte! Is it you? You must forgive!
CHARLOTTE:	I, forgive you? When 'tis I that have killed you, When the blood that is pouring from your wounds Was shed by me!
WERTHER:	No, what you have done is good, is right. My soul will bless you always for this death, Which has kept you stainless, and has spared me remorse.

As this grim scene unfolds, voices of children can be heard from outside.

CHILDREN:	Noel! Noel! Noel! Noel! Noel! Jesus Christ from heaven unto us this day is given,

[3] Copyright 1960 by Leonard Bernstein.

Hear, oh hear that holy voice . . .
Joy is good in his sight!
Ev'ry one should be gay!
Ev'ry one should be glad!
Noel! Noel! Noel! Noel! Noel!

And as Werther dies, their cheerful voices become louder.

Many composers have made effective use of an offstage chorus. The first act of Mussorgsky's *Boris Godunov* begins with a haunting scene in which an elderly monk, Pimen, sits in his cell in a monastery at night, writing a history of Russia. The voices of other monks are heard in the distance, singing the midnight office; they waken the young Gregory, who has been dreaming, and they continue intermittently as a background to the conversation which follows between Gregory and Pimen. They contribute to the mood of the scene: sombre, dark, rather foreboding. The effect is one peculiar to opera—we see one place, while the chorus singing offstage gives the impression of another. It is as though we are given a glimpse of a second set.

Another striking example of precisely the same effect comes at the beginning of Gounod's *Faust*. Again we have an aging man sitting at a table writing; it is Faust, the scholar, long isolated from most human emotions. From offstage we hear first a women's chorus, then men, then both, singing of the joys of nature and love. Faust tries to shut out the sounds, to forget his memories of human pleasures, but he cannot. The set represents a gloomy, musty study. Even though we do not see what is outside, the sound of the chorus and their text bring a mental picture of quite a different world from the one we see. Again, momentarily, the offstage chorus has given the impression of another setting, another mood.

THE CHORUS AS SOUND

Often a composer will decide that a certain section of his opera will be more impressive if he adds a chorus to his orchestra and whatever singers are involved in the scene, and he will write for the chorus in such a way that they merely amplify the sound, without having musical or dramatic material of their own.

In the first act of Bizet's *Carmen*, a crowd of young men has been waiting outside of a cigarette factory for the girls, particularly Carmen, to finish work. Carmen comes out and is greeted with shouts and questions, to which she replies in recitative. ("When will I love you? I don't know, maybe never! Maybe tomorrow! But not today, that much is certain.") Now she begins what has become one of the most famous tunes in the literature of opera, the *Habanera*, imitative of a Spanish song, depicting the character of Carmen: flirtatious, worldly, brash, confident. She begins alone, as though beginning an aria.

But after she has sung the first section, of 16 measures, the chorus echoes 8 measures of her song, with the same music and text, while Carmen sings fragments against them.

Now Carmen begins a contrasting phrase, also 16 measures in length. She sings most of this alone, though the chorus twice has exclama-

CARMEN

L'a-mour est en - fant de Bo - hême, Il n'a ja - mais, ja-mais con-nu de loi,

tions when she pauses for breath. The chorus now sings the first half of this second strain, and Carmen finishes it off by singing the last 8 measures. The first part of the song is repeated, with Carmen singing 16 measures and the chorus 8, then Carmen sings the 16 measures of the second section again, and the Habanera ends with Carmen and the chorus dividing the last section again, 8 measures apiece.

The chorus, then, merely repeats what the soloist has already sung. It has no music or text of its own, no personality of its own, no contribution to make to the drama at this point. The musical and dramatic effect of the scene would be the same if the sections sung by the chorus were eliminated, or sung by Carmen. The chorus contributes nothing but sonority, and is used at this point only because the composer decided that the scene would be more attractive with an additional sound element to contrast with the solo voice and the orchestra.

The judgment scene in the last act of Verdi's *Aida* is constructed as a duet, dramatically. Amneris is in a hall in the King's palace; priests, led by the High Priest Ramphis, go to the dungeon below, where Radames is held, and their voices can be heard accusing Radames of crimes against his country and then sentencing him to remain entombed under the altar. Amneris, hearing them, despairingly cries out against fate, and wildly accuses the priests of an inhuman act when they emerge from the dungeon. Thus there are two vividly contrasting elements: Amneris—distraught, frantic; and the priests—solemn, dignified, determined to carry out what they consider justice against a traitor. Verdi makes a sharp differentia-

*A choral scene from Wagner's Parsifal, as produced by
Indiana University in 1965.*

tion between the music sung by the two. Amneris has an agitated, restless melodic line.

Ramphis and the other priests share the same text and music, sometimes singing their solemn, stately phrases together,

and sometimes echoing one another.

The dramatic structure of the scene would have been precisely the same if Ramphis alone had entered, gone below and pronounced sentence on Radames, and emerged to sing the final portion of the scene with Amneris. Again the chorus has no musical or dramatic identity—it is nothing more than amplification of Ramphis. It is used in this scene only because Verdi sensed that a group of male voices singing in unison would be more imposing in sound, and contrast more strikingly with the soprano, than a single bass voice.

As was pointed out in the previous chapter, many composers are particularly fond of using the chorus in their finales. An act, or an entire opera, can suffer if the finale does not reach some musical and/or dramatic climax, and composers often insure against this by massing all possible musical forces on stage for a finale which is overwhelming in sheer sound. Usually the chorus is merely part of the general din, singing the same music and text as the principals. Rossini's *Barber of Seville* ends in this way; the plot has been resolved to the satisfaction of most of the participants, everyone possible is brought on stage, and the chorus's function is simply to contribute to the mass of sound.

THE CHORUS AS NARRATOR AND COMMENTATOR

When a composer uses his chorus as scenery, or as mere sound, the text is usually of no importance, and nothing will be lost if it is not understood. Americans, attending an opera in a language which they do not understand, tend to respond best to these uses of the chorus. But they are by no means the only ways in which composers have used chorus in their operas, and often small or even large parts of the dramatic framework will be lost if the text sung by the chorus cannot be comprehended, for whatever reason.

Bellini uses his chorus in the last act of *Lucia di Lammermoor* in a somewhat different manner than we have seen to this point. Lucy loves Edgar, but has been forced to marry Arthur. The second scene of the act takes place at the castle of Sir Henry Ashton, where the wedding has just taken place. The guests are enjoying a post-nuptial party, when suddenly Raymond enters:

CHORUS: Pale and breathless he appears!
What hath happened?
Ah, what is't? what hath befall'n?

Raymond, in dramatic accompanied recitative, tells how he has just come from Lucy's room, where he saw her, to his horror, kneeling by the body of her bridegroom, whom she had just stabbed.

CHORUS: Oh! dire misfortune, oh day of sorrow,
What gloomy ending of happy morrow!
Night, cast thy shadow o'er our lamenting,
Soon free her spirit from bonds of earth.

Raymond now says that the events of the day, and her crime, have driven her out of her mind.

CHORUS: Oh heav'n in mercy the crime forgive her,
Sad was her fate, cruel hatred's prey.

Lucy enters, in a white gown, pale and obviously mad,

CHORUS: Oh sight of sorrow,
As from the grave arisen.

and sings the first part of her famous "mad scene." With much coloratura flourish, she reminisces about her happy hours with her true love, Edgar. When she finally stops for breath, the chorus comments:

CHORUS: Oh, send her relief, kind heaven!
Poor maiden, true to the faith she vow'd!

Henry Ashton enters, and there is some recitative and a brief trio.

CHORUS: Unhappy maid! Heav'n behold and end her woe!
Oh, night of grief and doom!

Lucy's coloratura antics become even more breathtaking as she gives instructions for her burial, and this section of the act ends with the three principals singing against the chorus's final comments.

CHORUS: Short were thy days of pleasure,
Grief stole thy life away, unhappy one.[4]

The text sung by the chorus may not be of great dramatic importance, but the chorus has a personality of its own. It reacts to what it sees and hears, and comments on what is happening, expressing precisely the emotions which the composer hopes the audience is experiencing.

When the chorus is used to offer commentary in an operatic scene, it often sings text which, while it may not move the drama forward, is important for the audience to comprehend. It may serve as a foil for whatever the principals are singing, or it may be a text on which the poet has lavished care, which is rich in images, which represents the most beautiful poetry he can write. Many poets are conscious of the tradition of the chorus in Greek drama, and fashion choral sections which reflect what they understand of this ancient art.

Composers have sometimes used their chorus in narrative style, to offer information which the audience should have in order to follow the drama. Gounod does this at the very beginning of his *Romeo and Juliet:* the curtain goes up in the middle of the overture, to reveal the entire cast of principals lined up across the stage facing the audience.

CHORUS: Two households, noble both, in Verona's fair city,
From ancient grudge break to new fray,
Civil blood now is shed, without remorse or pity:
On this we found the traffic of our play.[5]

Two more verses complete the sketching-in of the situation, the curtain falls, the orchestra finishes off the overture, and the first act begins. This is narration, and the composer has set it in syllabic, note-against-note style to insure that the audience understands every word. It could be called choral recitative.

[4] Translation by Natalia Macfarren.
[5] Translation by Dr. Theodore Baker.

The point might be raised that any audience can be expected to know the story of Romeo and Juliet so well that it makes no difference whether or not this prologue is understood. But every successful play has been written with the assumption that the audience does not know what will happen, that every dramatic point must be made clear to them, and every successful production starts from the same assumption. This is true, of course, even of present-day productions of plays of the recent and distant past—including those of Shakespeare. A production of his *Romeo and Juliet* in which lines are lost and dramatic points obscured would be assailed by critics and rejected by audiences, and the director would be laughed at if he attempted to defend himself on the grounds that "everyone knows what happens anyway." The same standard should be applied to operatic productions.

Aaron Copland planned his *The Second Hurricane* to be done on a bare stage, completely without sets, with the soloists and choruses sitting on simple wooden benches. There is little physical action; the plot is carried forward mostly by narration, much of it by chorus. For example, this chorus shortly after the beginning of the second act paints a picture which is not seen on the stage and offers information which is new:

WOMEN: Butch, Fat, Gyp and Lowrie, Gwen, Queenie and Jeff,
They're safe on Two Willow Hill.
Safe in the midst of the flood.
Together in the dark of night.

MEN: Safe? No, they are not safe,
They are not safe yet.

WOMEN: Nobody knows where they landed,
Nobody knows where they are.

BOTH: Nobody knows yet that they're in the midst of the flood,
That around them a flood is rising, rising,
Rising in the dark of night.
Search-planes are flying,
But they can't find the hill.
Search-planes are dropping light-flares,
But all they light up is a waste of flood.

Butch, Fat, Gyp and Lowrie, Gwen and Queenie and Jeff.
Nobody knows where they are lost.
Search-planes could find them on their little island,
But by morning—there won't be any island left.
There won't be any Two-Willow Hill.
In the dark of the night the water is rising still.[6]

This is pure narration, and the chorus must be as careful with its diction as the composer was in setting the text, or the entire point of the scene will be lost.

[6] Copyright 1938 by Aaron Copland; renewed 1965. Reprinted by permission of Aaron Copland, copyright owner, and Boosey and Hawkes, Inc., sole publishers.

The second act of Gluck's *Orfeo* begins with Orfeo entering the underworld, in an attempt to find Euridice and bring her back with him. His way is barred by a chorus of Furies:

FURIES: Who is this mortal one
Now drawing near to this region of gloominess,
Bold to intrude on these awful abodes?
(they dance)
Deadly affright and amazement take hold of him,
While on his entering, dreadful and menacing
    Cerebus waits.

Gluck has set this text in a simple, syllabic, note-against-note manner so that the audience will have no difficulty comprehending what is sung.

Orfeo plays on his lyre (a harp sounds from the orchestra) and pleads his case:

ORFEO: O be merciful to me, furies, spectres, phantoms . . .
FURIES: No! no! no!
ORFEO: O let your hearts have pity on my soul-tormenting pain . . .

FURIES: No! no! no!
ORFEO: O be merciful to me . . .
FURIES: No! . . .

The Furies, less menacing now, caution him:

FURIES: Sorrowing mortal, in this place what seekest thou?
Gloom as of midnight, and moaning, and crying,
Abide in this sphere of affliction and terror.
Mortal, what seekest thou? What?
Here is the dwelling of death's fearful agony,
Here only wailing is, here are but pangs.

Orfeo sings another stanza of his plea ("Thousand tortures, phantoms of terror, are to me . . ."), and the Furies are by now quite moved:

FURIES: What feeling, strange to us, tender and pitiful,
Checks our resistance, inclines us to mercy,
And melts our hearts?

Another stanza by Orfeo ("My entreating, my complaining, would at length your pity move, Had ye ever felt the anguish of the loss of one ye love") has the Furies almost in tears, and they capitulate and allow him to pass:

FURIES: His moving elegies, his mournful melodies,
Waken our sympathy, meekly appeal to us, master our will!
Therefore, ye gates, we command you, unclose yourselves,
Into the underworld entrance we grant to him,
He has prevailed! [7]

The chorus of Furies is not merely part of the scenery or sound, nor does it comment on what others have said or done. Its text is not extraneous to the dramatic development of the scene; if it were omitted, the scene would make no sense. The chorus, collectively, is one of the characters in the drama. It begins in one emotional state and in the course of the scene is transformed to another. It has a distinct personality, its own text, its own part to play in the drama. It is one of the protagonists.

Mussorgsky's *Boris Godunov* is filled with choruses of this sort, so much so that it is often said that the chorus, representing the Russian people, is in fact the central figure of the entire opera. This use of the chorus as protagonist can be traced back almost to the very beginning of opera: Monteverdi's *L'Incoronazione di*

[7] Translation by Rev. J. Troutbeck.

Poppea has an effective and moving scene in which Seneca announces that Nero's actions have made it necessary for him to kill himself, and his students plead with him not to do it.

Wagner's *The Flying Dutchman* contains a remarkable scene, the first of the third act, made up entirely of three choruses. The set depicts two ships at anchor: one, Norwegian, with sailors dancing and singing on deck; the other a Dutch ship, silent and dark. The crew of the first ship sings:

NORWEGIAN SAILORS:

>Steersman, leave the watch! Steersman, come away!
>Ho! He! Je! Ha! Make the anchor fast!
>Furl the sails! Steersman, come!
>What care we for wind or tide?
>Here we'll sit and sing so fine,
>With our sweethearts by our side,
>Good tobacco, and fiery wine!

After they dance for a bit, a group of girls enters, carrying food and drink. They tease the Norwegians by pretending that they will take the refreshments to the Dutch ship.

GIRLS: Now, look! look! look! They're dancing there!
          No need for us, I do declare!

NORWEGIAN SAILORS: Hey! Maidens! Here! this is the way!

GIRLS: How would you like some wine today?

The girls, now curious about the Dutch ship, shout up to it.

GIRLS: Hey! Sailors! hey! Speak, where are ye?
          Show us a light! we cannot see!

The Norwegians join the girls in shouting, and the two choruses sing together ("Sailors! Sailors! awake!") When there is no answer, the girls become frightened (" 'Tis true, then, the men are dead! They have no need of wine or bread."), give their baskets to the Norwegians, and hurry off. The sailors open them, are delighted to find wine, and resume their boisterous singing.

Now a wind begins whistling around the Dutch ship and a strange blue fire burns on the mast, lighting up members of the crew who sing a curious, ominous song.

DUTCH SAILORS: Jo-ho-hoe! Jo-ho-ho-hoe! Ho-jo-ho-hoe! Hoe!
                 Through the storm, to the shore, Huissa!
                 Furl the sails, anchor down, Huissa!

Gloomy captain, haste to land,
Now the seven long years are o'er!
Woo and win a maiden's hand,
Maid, be faithful evermore! [8]

As they sing, the wind builds up around their ship, until a
storm is raging, even though the rest of the sea is calm. The
Norwegian sailors are terrified, but attempt to drown out the
sounds coming from the Dutch vessel by singing their own song
more loudly ("Steersman, leave the watch!"). For a bit, the two
choruses sing against one another, but the wind and the song
coming from the Dutch ship soon silence the Norwegian crew.
Terrified, they go below, making the sign of the cross. At this,
wild screams of laughter come from the Dutch ship, then suddenly
the storm ceases, the light goes out, and the strange ship is as
quiet and as dark as it was at the beginning of the scene.

There are, in effect, three protagonists in this scene—the three
choruses. Except for a few unimportant phrases sung by the steersman of the Norwegian ship, the scene is built completely around
what is sung by these choruses.

Rossini makes highly effective use of multiple chorus in the
finale of the second act of his *William Tell*. Three Swiss patriots
(Tell, Arnold, and Walter) have met in a pine forest at night to
plot a revolt against the occupying Austrians and the brutal Governor
of Switzerland, Gesler. After an extended trio, the three hear
footsteps approaching and the men of the village of Unterwald enter,
answering Tell's challenge by identifying themselves as patriots.

Now trumpets sound, and the men of Switz enter.

[8] Translation by Rev. J. Troutbeck and Dr. Theodore Baker.

Tell welcomes them. Another group approaches, is challenged, and identifies itself as the men of Uri, also *"Amici della patria!"* The three choruses sing together of their patriotism and their desire to free their country from foreign oppression.

Tell exhorts them further, and they all clasp hands and take an oath to fight against tyranny, the three choruses and three principals singing together in one of the most thrilling scenes in all opera. Although a static dramatic point is reached at the end as everyone joins in an overwhelming mass of sound, the effect of the scene is of six protagonists, the three principals and the three choruses.

❦ SUMMARY

Composers have found a variety of ways to use their chorus. It may temporarily take over tasks normally assigned to solo singers, presenting new information in narrative style, or reflecting on what has taken place. But it may do many other things, as well. Often it is merely part of the stage picture, helping to establish the time and locale of the action, or setting an appropriate mood for what is to take place. At other times it is used as an element of sound, having no music or text of its own but merely singing along with one or more of the principals, creating a more impressive mass of sound. This often happens in finales, where composers like to amass the most formidable musical forces possible. At other times the chorus observes what is said and done on stage and offers commentary on it, acting as a sort of vocal audience. Many of the best composers have not been content with using the chorus as a passive element, but have constructed scenes in which it takes on a distinct personality, playing part in the development of the drama.

VII

THE ORCHESTRA
AND ITS USE

Most of the basic concepts and techniques of opera cut across the boundaries established when the history of music is sectionalized into various periods (Baroque, Classical, Romantic, and Contemporary). Distinction between recitative and aria has been present in opera from its beginnings right up to the present, and the reasons for the distinction are the same in an opera by Mozart as in one by Purcell or Verdi or Britten. Composers have used a chorus in their operas from the early seventeenth century to the present, and in similar ways. The more one studies the structure of opera, the more one is impressed with the continuity of form and with the fact that certain techniques of the earliest composers have served ever since.

Not so with the operatic orchestra, and its use. The makeup of the orchestra in the early days of opera was quite different from the orchestra later in the eighteenth century, which in turn was unlike that of Wagner and Strauss. The function of the orchestra has likewise changed dramatically. There has been more change in the orchestra—its size, personnel, and function—than in any other aspect of opera, and since these changes have followed a clear chronological pattern, this one chapter will be developed in historical sequence.

BEGINNINGS: THE CONTINUO AND THE SINGER

The earliest operas, those written by members of the Florentine Camerata at the end of the sixteenth century and beginning of the seventeenth, were conceived more as dramatic works than as musical ones. Nevertheless they were sung throughout, and there was an orchestra.

Peri's *Euridice* of 1600 used four instruments, hidden behind a screen so as not to distract the singers and audience. This was a curious orchestra by modern standards: a *gravicembalo* (harpsichord), a *chitarrone* (large lute), a *liuto grosso* (another large lute), and a *lira grande* (a bowed stringed instrument). Not one was a melody-playing instrument. The score from which they played consisted of nothing more than a bass line, with occasional indications as to what chord should be played.

La-cri - ma te al mio pian - to om - bre d'in-fer - no.

The *lira* played this line, while one or more of the other instruments played chords to accompany the singers. The exact notes in these chords, and the rhythm in which they were to be played, were left to the discretion of the performers. These were quiet instruments, the harpsichord making less noise than even an upright piano, and the lutes capable of not much more sound than a modern (unamplified) guitar. Such an orchestra could do no more than furnish a light chordal background, with a more solid bass line, for the singer. Even a light voice could carry over them, and the slightest nuance of expressive singing or ornamentation of any sort would be perceptible.

The foundation of seventeenth-century instrumental music was the *basso continuo:* one or more low-pitched instruments (usually strings) playing the bass line and one or more chord-playing instruments improvising a harmonic skein above them. The written part from which the basso continuo was realized was called the *figured bass.* The basso continuo formed a rhythmic and harmonic groundwork for all music of this period—operatic, orchestral, instrumental —against which solo singers or instrumentalists played their parts. It furnished a light support, just enough to sketch in the basic harmonies and rhythmic patterns, but never enough to intrude on or compete with the soloists. It has often been likened to the "rhythm section" of a modern dance band or jazz group—a bass, a piano, and maybe a guitar and drummer giving the "beat" and chord progressions against which melody instruments play their parts.

To the Camerata, a good singer was one who could project a text expressively and embroider the written vocal line with delicate and emotional ornamentation. The quiet support of a *continuo* group was all that was needed in the way of an orchestra.

🐜 MONTEVERDI AND EXPANSION OF THE ORCHESTRA

From a glance at the list of instruments used by Claudio Monteverdi in his *Orfeo*, written only a few years later (1607), we can see that he had quite different ideas about orchestration. It must be remembered that this opera was not written to be performed in a room in a private home for the benefit of a handful of intellectuals, but for festive performance in a large hall in a palace, for a quite sizable audience. Monteverdi calls for:

2 gravicembali (harpsichords)
2 contrabassi da viola (double-bass viols)
10 viole da braccio (viols, held in the arms)
1 arpa doppia (double harp)
2 violini piccoli alla Francese (violins)
2 chitarroni (large lutes)
2 organi di legno (organs with wooden pipes)
3 bassi da gamba (bass viols)
4 tromboni (trombones)
1 regale (portable organ)
2 cornetti (cornetts)
1 flautino alla vigesima seconda (recorder)
1 clarino con tre trombe sordine (1 high trumpet, 3 "soft" trumpets)
arpe (harp)
1 ceteroni (cittern)
3 flautini (recorders)

Here we are in another world of orchestral practice, with a collection of instruments as large and varied as that used in many modern orchestras. But the makeup of this group, and Monteverdi's use of the various instruments and families of instruments, is altogether different from the practice familiar to us from the current repertory. The most obvious difference is the wealth of chord-playing instruments in *Orfeo:* harpsichords, harps, lutes, organs, cittern. The most important difference, though, can be seen readily in the following chart of the first act:

SINGERS	TEXT BEGINNING	INSTRUMENTATION
a shepherd	*"In questo lieto"*	continuo
chorus (5-part)	*"Vieni Imeneo"*	tutti (all instruments)
a nymph	*"Muse honor"*	continuo
chorus (5-part)	*"Lasciate i monti"*	5 viole da braccio, 3 chitarroni, 2 gravicembali, 1 arpa doppia, 1 contrabassi da viola, 1 flautino
instrumental ritornello A		5 unspecified instruments
a shepherd	*"Ma tu gentil"*	continuo
Orfeo	*"Rosa del ciel"*	continuo
Euridice	*"Io non diro"*	continuo
chorus (5-part)	*"Lasciate i monti"*	as above
instrumental ritornello A		5 unspecified instruments
chorus (5-part)	*"Vieni Imeneo"*	tutti
a shepherd	*"Ma s'il nostro"*	continuo
instrumental ritornello B		5 unspecified instruments
duet (shepherds)	*"Alcun non sia"*	continuo
instrumental ritornello B		5 unspecified instruments
trio (shepherds)	*"Che poi"*	continuo
instrumental ritornello B		5 unspecified instruments
duet (shepherds)	*"È dopo l'astro"*	continuo
chorus (5-part)	*"Ecco Orfeo"*	5 unspecified instruments
instrumental sinfonia		5 unspecified instruments

Despite the size of the orchestra, solo singers (singing alone, or in duets or trios) are accompanied only by a basso continuo. With the wealth of chord-playing instruments available, we can guess that the sound of this accompaniment was variable: now a harp, now an organ, now a harpsichord, now several of these together. In fact, in the later acts Monteverdi does specify, several times, which of these instruments is to play the continuo in a particular scene. But whichever instruments were used at a given

*Male chorus in Wagner's The Flying Dutchman,
Act I. Bayreuth, 1959.*

The Opera Company of Boston

A scene from Offenbach's Tales of Hoffman, as produced by The Opera Company of Boston.

French Cultural Services

Photo Bernard

A ballet scene from the Paris Opera production of Arthur Honneger's L'Aiglon.

A production of Verdi's Don Carlos at the Paris Opera.

moment, they furnished a quiet, subdued, completely subordinate accompaniment for the singers, in no way competing or compelling the performer to sing with more volume or force.

The other instruments are used to accompany the chorus, or to play ritornelli (short instrumental sections inserted between vocal numbers) and sinfonias (more extended instrumental sections, usually found at the beginnings or ends of acts).

Monteverdi wrote for a variety of soloists and a richly varied orchestra—but not for both together. For him, as for the members of the Camerata, the solo voice was to be supported as lightly as possible, with continuo only. Monteverdi was quite aware of the

dramatic effects possible from a contrast of various instruments and groups of instruments. The ritornelli in the pastoral scenes of the first act use flutes; the scenes in the underworld later in the opera have heavier and darker instrumentation (a chorus of spirits, for example, sings to the accompaniment of the regal, 5 trombones, 2 bass viols, and a double-bass viol); in the final act, Orfeo and Apollo ascend to the skies to the sound of strings, harps, and other plucked instruments. But these instruments are never used simultaneously with the soloists.

In the one section in which a solo voice and instruments are used together, Orfeo's extended aria *"Possente spirito"* in the third act, the two still do not compete. The singer is accompanied, as always, by the basso continuo, and the other instruments play only between the soloist's phrases, as shown on page 129.

LATER SEVENTEENTH-CENTURY PRACTICE

Cesti's *Il Pomo d'Oro*, performed in Vienna in 1667 for the wedding of the Emperor Leopold I, was one of the most spectacular stage productions of the entire century. Elaborate sets, designed by Lodovico Burnacini, depicted gods descending from the heavens on clouds, battles on sea and land, violent storms, and other dramatic and colorful events. The score called for several dozen soloists, a large chorus, and what was, for those days, a large orchestra: 6 violins; 4 each of alto, tenor, and bass viols; a contrabass viol; bassoons; cornetts; trumpets; trombones; cembalo (harpsichord); theorbo (bass lute); and archiliuto (another variety of bass lute). The instruments were used for color and for dramatic effect: a scene at the entrance to Hell had a ritornello exploiting the sombre sound of cornetts, trombones, and bassoon; a scene in the palace of Job was introduced by a ritornello using the rich sound of a five-part string choir; martial and battle scenes used trumpets. Choruses were accompanied by large groups of instruments. The sound of such scenes was rich, full, massive, matching the grandeur of the sets and costumes. Yet whenever a solo singer performed, the orchestration was reduced to the quiet sound of the basso continuo alone.

On a few occasions, however, soloists and a few instruments other than the continuo were used together. Cesti handled this situation in one of two ways. Either the singer and the instruments were treated in antiphonal fashion, answering one another, or, in

a few highly emotional passages, the singer sang *with* a few other instruments. However, these played nothing more than simple sustaining chords, being in effect merely an extension of the basso continuo.

Jean-Baptiste Lully, the chief composer of opera in France at this time, worked his way into a position of eminence by his playing and directing of instrumental groups. He was a master conductor,

and it was generally admitted that the sounds which came from his orchestra far surpassed those heard in Italy. Yet his well-drilled strings and winds were reserved for the opening overture, for ritornelli, for the numerous dances in his works, and for an accompaniment for chorus. When a solo singer held the stage, Lully, like all composers of the time, rested his orchestra and supported the singer with only a basso continuo. Rarely, a singer would have some slight instrumental accompaniment—at most, a few strings playing simple chords, or a wind playing an obbligato part.

Large, colorful orchestras were usually reserved for festival operas. Many less pretentious works called for much smaller instrumental forces, sometimes only a string ensemble and a continuo. Carlo Pallavicini's *La Gerusalemme Liberata*, performed in Venice in 1687, was scored for: violin I, II; violetta I, II; viola da collo; basso; and cembalo.

This is quite a modest orchestra, capable of only limited volume and color. Even so, solo voices were mostly supported by continuo alone, the cembalo and the "basso," a low-pitched stringed instrument. On the few occasions when the strings were used with the voice, they played either in antiphonal fashion, as shown opposite, or in simple sustained chords.

There was no standardization of the orchestra in the seventeenth century; composers wrote for whatever instrumental forces were available, and an opera written in one city might call for a quite different group of players than one written for performance in another. Whatever instruments were available were used to play ritornelli, sinfonias, and dance music, and to accompany the chorus, but almost never to support the principals. This job was left to the basso continuo.

🕮 NEAPOLITAN OPERA AND SPECTACULAR SINGING

Some of the most spectacular singers in the entire history of opera were active in the last decades of the seventeenth century and first half of the eighteenth, singing Italian operas which were gradually shedding chorus, dance, and other extraneous elements in the increasing fascination with virtuoso solo singing. This was the era of the Metastasian libretto, of what has been somewhat confusingly called Neapolitan opera, which was made up largely of a succession of recitatives and solo arias. This was the age of such famous artists as Senesino, Farinelli, Bordoni, Faustini, and Boschi.

It was said that Farinelli engaged in a public competition with a trumpet player and outdid even this noisiest of instruments in both range and volume. But the art of these singers was by no means based on loud and high voices. Time and again, we hear of a singer praised for his expressiveness and for the variety and facility of the ornamentation with which he embroidered the melodic line given him by the composer. Singing teachers were supposed to teach the art of ornamentation, to furnish their students with notebooks containing the various figures which could be used to ornament the arias they would sing.

The most popular aria type of the time was the *da capo*, in ABA form. In modern performances of such arias it is often tedious to hear a singer perform a second time, note for note, what he has already sung once as the first part of the aria. But not then. The repetition was anything but literal—the whole idea of a *da capo* aria was that a singer would sing the A section once in a reasonably straightforward way, and would show his skill and agility by applying as much ornamentation as he felt was appropriate, and of which he was capable, when he repeated it.

The orchestra in this period was still built around the basso continuo, and was still variable in size and personnel. It played an overture or opening sinfonia, sometimes other sinfonias in the course of the opera, and ballet music if there was any. The ritornello had largely disappeared, or rather had become the introduction to an aria. Some arias were still accompanied by the continuo alone, but as the eighteenth century wore on, it became more the fashion for the composer to write other instrumental parts to accompany his arias. By mid-century, a singer could expect to sing most of his arias with instruments in addition to the continuo.

The trend toward accompanied arias is illustrated in the following chart of the arias and ariosos in the first part of the second act of Handel's *Agrippina*, performed in Venice in 1709. Recitative is still accompanied by basso continuo, but there is much more variety in the orchestration of arias.

CHARACTER	TEXT BEGINNING	ACCOMPANIMENT
Ottone	*"Coronato il crin"*	violins, viola, continuo
Chorus	*"Di timpani e trombe"*	2 trumpets, timpani, violins, 2 oboes, viola, continuo
Claudio	*"Cade il mondo"*	violins (unison), continuo
Agrippina	*"Nulla sperarda me"*	continuo
Poppea	*"Tuo ben"*	continuo
Nerone	*"Sotto il lauro"*	violins (unison), viola, continuo
Ottone	*"Voi che udite"*	oboe, 2 violins, viola, continuo
Poppea	*"Bella pur"*	2 oboes, 2 violins, viola, continuo (middle section: continuo alone)
Ottone	*"Vaghe fonti"*	2 flutes, 2 muted violins, viola, continuo
Ottone	*"Ti vo' giusta"*	continuo

The implications of the term *accompanied aria* as applied to opera of this period are misleading to us today. The operatic orchestra used in the early eighteenth century was far more modest in size than those of even the smallest opera houses today. Such an orchestra, of about a dozen pieces, is more like what we call a chamber orchestra today. Even if all the instruments were to play together, the sound would be nothing like that of a modern operatic orchestra. Moreover, the woodwind instruments were not capable of as much volume as their modern counterparts.

The entire orchestra was almost never used to accompany an aria. Composers used their instruments to accompany singers in one of several well-defined and limited ways, each designed to enrich the sound but to interfere as little as possible with the notes coming from the singers' throats, which were what everyone had come to hear.

Most typical was the obbligato accompaniment, in which an aria was scored for the singer, the continuo, and one or two additional instruments. The instrument would give out the first 8 or 16 measures of the melody, accompanied by the continuo; when the singer began it would continue to play, answering the vocalist in antiphonal or echo fashion or simply playing along in counterpoint or obbligato to the voice. We see this type of accompaniment in an aria from Handel's *Poro*.

sai che de-li - ra   spes-so si la - gna,

sem - pre so-spi - ra,—

It is scarcely accurate to speak of this as an accompanied aria. The actual accompaniment is furnished by the continuo; the solo instrument or instruments play the same sort of line as the voice is singing. The effect is more of a duet or trio, with the voice and one or two instruments competing on equal terms. With so few instruments, there is little danger of the singer being covered. Besides, dynamic markings were rarely put in the score; an instrumentalist was expected to be a good enough musician to adjust his volume to that of the singer.

When an aria was accompanied by a larger group of instruments, the composer usually fell back on the old trick of antiphonal writing, having the singer and instruments alternate, not compete. Sometimes at the climax of a phrase, when the voice was singing in its most favorable register, both would be used together, momentarily. Here again it is misleading to say that the instruments were accompanying the voice—they were mostly alternating with it. But occasionally we find an aria in which some of the instruments did play for long stretches while the singing was going on. Such a situation was inevitably treated carefully by the composer. The accompanying instruments would be selected from among the quieter ones of the orchestra, and they would play either simple chords, as in the aria from Handel's *Rinaldo* shown on page 138,

or simple, unobtrusive accompanimental figures, as in his *Ottone*, which would not detract from the vocal line. We can be sure that the dynamic level of such an accompaniment would be adjusted in rehearsal if it showed signs of competing with the voice. (See the example opposite.)

Much of what we know of singing styles of the past comes from a study of how instruments were used with solo voices, and it seems apparent that in this age of spectacular singing, voices must

have been clear, light, and extraordinarily flexible. Composers were careful not to cover their singers with even the modest instrumental means at their disposal. Soloists were mostly supported by a light continuo, and were expected to hold their own against obbligato solo instruments and sometimes light chords from the orchestra, but no composer would have asked his singers to compete against all of the instruments assembled in the pit. The art of singing was such that no artist was expected to match, in volume, the modest-sized orchestras of the day.

Until the second half of the eighteenth century, there was no standardization of the opera orchestra. One in Paris might have 20 strings and woodwinds and brasses by twos; an Italian orchestra in a small town might have only strings—and only 8 or 10 of these—and harpsichord; the Hamburg orchestra might be weak in strings but have 5 flutes, 4 oboes, 5 bassoons, 4 horns and trumpets, and a drum. Operas written for one city were rarely performed elsewhere, and when this did happen, the composer (or someone else) would often have to reorchestrate the work for the particular collection of instruments available.

But this situation changed. Composers in all parts of Europe—Haydn, Mozart, Gluck, Sammartini, Stamitz, Méhul—began writing for an orchestra which was basically the same. A five-part string section was its heart (violin I, violin II, viola, cello, and double bass), augmented by pairs of flutes, oboes, bassoons, horns, sometimes trumpets, and later clarinets. There was still some variation in size, and occasionally other instruments were used for one reason or another, but as the century neared an end it became more and more possible for works written for one city to be performed in another.

Selecting at random from Mozart's operas, we see that he wrote for basically the same orchestra in each:

La Finta Semplice (Vienna, 1768)	2 flutes, 2 oboes, 2 bassoons, 2 horns, strings
Ascanio in Alba (Milan, 1771)	2 flutes, 2 oboes, 2 bassoons, 2 horns, 2 trumpets, timpani, strings
Idomeneo (Munich, 1781)	2 flutes, 2 oboes, 2 clarinets, 2 bassoons, 4 horns, 2 trumpets, 3 trombones, timpani, strings
Figaro (Vienna, 1786)	2 flutes, 2 oboes, 2 clarinets, 2 bassoons, 2 horns, 2 trumpets, timpani, strings
Don Giovanni (Prague, 1787)	2 flutes, 2 oboes, 2 clarinets, 2 bassoons, 2 horns, 2 trumpets, 3 trombones, timpani, strings

With this standardization came a significant change: the replacement of the basso continuo as the foundation of the orchestra by the string choir. The harpsichord was part of the orchestra throughout most of the eighteenth century, and still accompanied secco recitative, but elsewhere—in arias, duets, ensembles, choruses, dances, and overtures—the string choir was the core of the orchestra.

For the first time in the history of opera the orchestra was normally used to accompany solo singers, in arias and ensembles. For the first time, singers were asked to sing *with* the orchestra. This was a fundamental change in the use of the orchestra in opera.

Mostly the singers were supported by simple figures, in effect little different from the sort of accompaniment furnished by the basso continuo, as seen in this excerpt from an aria for Dorabella in Mozart's *Così fan Tutte*.

To be sure, this change did not affect the singer too much at first. Orchestras were still small, by present-day standards, and singing with them was not the same thing as singing with a modern orchestra. A picture of Haydn directing a performance of one of his operas at Esterház shows 12 violins and violas, 3 lower strings, 3 wind players, and a harpsichord—19 players in all. The orchestra for the first performance of Mozart's *Figaro* in Prague was composed of 25 players: 3 first violins, 4 seconds, 2 violas, 1 cello, 2 basses, 2 flutes, 2 oboes, 2 clarinets, 2 bassoons, 2 horns, 2 trumpets, and a drum. Even this figure is misleading; much of the time Mozart accompanies his singers with only strings, a mere dozen players in this instance.

But even simple passages had more body than a continuo, necessitating some adjustments in the technique of the singer. And not infrequently, when the composer wanted a climax of sound during an aria or ensemble, he used most or all of his orchestra at a loud dynamic level. The example opposite is from Gluck's *Alceste*.

Something quite new in the history of opera is happening in such a passage: the singer must be capable of enough volume to be heard in competition with twenty or thirty instruments. He can no longer sing at a dynamic level which pleases him; he must make enough sound to be heard over the orchestra—and if he is not capable of this, he is not suited for the part. Though the normal function of the orchestra in the operas of Mozart, Gluck, and their contemporaries is to support the singer, to accompany him, it may on occasion compete with him. A new requirement has been added to the skills necessary for the operatic singer.

🕮 THE NINETEENTH CENTURY AND THE GIANT ORCHESTRA

The clear pattern emerging from this discussion of the changing orchestra in the opera pit is of a steadily increasing group used in more ways in the course of an opera, and this pattern continues in the nineteenth century.

More and larger groups of instruments were used. Winds often used by fours, rather than pairs, and new instruments such as the English horn, bass clarinet, contrabassoon, and saxophone were introduced. Mechanical improvements were made in the woodwind and brass instruments, giving them more flexibility and, in some instances, more volume. Though there were no technical changes in the strings, with the use of more and better winds it was

necessary to increase the size of the string choir to maintain a satisfactory balance.

Spontini's orchestra in Berlin in the 1820's had 12 first and 12 second violins, 8 violas, 9 celli, and 7 basses—a total of 48 strings—and Habeneck's Paris orchestra in 1828 had strings by 15, 16, 8, 12, and 8, adding up to 59. The orchestra at Covent Garden in 1848 had 61 strings (16,15,10,10,10), and by 1880 the Vienna Philharmonic had a string section of 77 (20,20,16,12,9).

Even these orchestras, mammoth by standards of the seventeenth and eighteenth centuries, were dwarfed by the forces assembled for festivals and other special occasions. For a concert of Beethoven's music in Vienna in 1814, 79 strings were used (18,18,14,12,17) and a corresponding number of winds. Verdi used an orchestra of 100 and a chorus of 120 for the first performance of his *Requiem* in 1874, but even this could not match the forces assembled for Berlioz's *Messe des Morts* in 1837: hundreds of singers, an orchestra of 110 strings, comparable winds and percussion, and four different brass bands placed in various corners of the church. The same composer is said to have used a 300-voice choir and a 500-piece orchestra for his *Damnation of Faust* and *Harold in Italy* in Vienna in 1866. Gustav Mahler's Eighth Symphony was called the "Symphony of a Thousand," in only slight exaggeration of the number of performers necessary for its enormously augmented orchestra and two mixed choruses.

The passion for gigantic instrumental forces touched even the New World. Theodore Thomas mustered the following players for the New York Music Festival of 1882.

> 6 harps
> 2 piccolos, 6 flutes
> 7 oboes, 2 English horns
> 6 clarinets, 2 bass clarinets
> 6 bassoons, 2 contrabassoons
> 9 French horns, 2 saxhorns
> 11 cornets, 3 trumpets, 1 bass trumpet
> 9 trombones, 3 tubas
> 50 1st violins
> 50 2nd violins
> 36 violas
> 36 celli
> 40 basses

These orchestras were used for the performance of orchestral music, often with chorus, but opera orchestras grew at almost the same rate. The orchestra of the Opera in Paris numbered 20 strings and 8 winds in 1713 but had tripled by 1855: 48 strings (11, 11, 8, 10, 8,); 3 each of flutes, clarinets, oboes and bassoons; 5 horns; 4 trumpets; 4 trombones; and timpani. La Scala, the famous opera house in Milan, had a string section of 50 by 1816 (12, 12, 10, 8, 8), and the Berlin opera in 1841 had 54 strings (14, 14, 8, 10, 8), woodwinds by fours, and 4 horns. An orchestra of 90 and a chorus of 120 were used for the production of Verdi's *Aida* in Milan in 1872.

Verdi's Aida, in a production by the Indiana University Opera Theater.

Wagner specified in his later operas that the string section should number 64 (16, 16, 12, 12, 8); an orchestra of 116 players was used for the first Bayreuth festival in 1876. Richard Strauss's *Elektra*, written in the early years of the twentieth century but representing a continuation of nineteenth-century practice, requires the following players.

4 flutes, 4 oboes

8 clarinets, 4 bassoons

4 French horns, 4 tubas

6 trumpets, 6 bass trumpets

4 trombones, 1 contrabass tuba

6-8 kettledrums

glockenspiel, triangle, tambourine, bass drum, cymbals, tamtam, celesta, 2 harps

24 violins (divided into 1st, 2nd, and 3rd)

18 violas (divided into 1st, 2nd, and 3rd)

12 celli (divided into 1st and 2nd)

8 basses

This is a far cry from the four quiet instruments supporting the singers in Peri's opera of 1600—and even from the two dozen or so players used by Mozart and Haydn.

Having given themselves such a large and varied orchestra, composers were faced with the problem of what uses to make of it. First, of course, they used it in the ways orchestras had been used in earlier operas: to play preliminary music before acts, to accompany the chorus, to play dance music, and to play introductions to arias and ensembles and then accompany the singers in the course of such numbers. And this rich orchestra often worked quite well in accompaniment. With such a variety of instruments available, such a large palette of orchestral color to choose from, composers could select single instruments, or small groups of them, so as to have an almost infinite range of sound for accompaniments.

If the orchestra were handled discreetly and selectively, the relationship between it and the singer would be very much the same as it had been in the previous century. The better operatic composers knew how to treat the orchestra with restraint, how to choose among the instruments those that would not infringe on the sound of the voice, how to accompany singers now with this group, now with that, achieving variety and reserving massed orchestral sounds for appropriate moments. But so many players sitting in the pit were a temptation that no composer of the time could resist for too long a stretch. As the century wore on, composers began to use most and sometimes all of this huge orchestra at the slightest provocation, no matter who was singing, and singers were asked, with increasing frequency, to do something which they had never been asked to do before—sing *against* an orchestra of as many as a hundred instruments, as in the passage from Verdi's *Aida* shown on page 148.

The first requirement for a singer who was asked to sing such a passage was the ability simply to make as much or more noise as the orchestra, to be heard over the uproar of so many instruments, and to have the physical strength and stamina to do it repeatedly over a span of three or four hours. Entirely new methods of producing a vocal tone were necessary.

It might be noted at this point that exactly the same thing was happening in the instrumental form of the concerto. A violinist or keyboard player performing a Bach or Mozart concerto was accompanied, in his solo passages, by a continuo or light string chords, or played in antiphonal fashion with the other instruments. By the end of the nineteenth century, a soloist was often asked to play *against* the sound of sixty or eighty other instruments. Great physical strength became a new requirement for a concert pianist.

The term *bel canto* is used to describe a technique of singing which stresses a light, flexible, pure, agile line. It supposedly developed in the eighteenth century in Italian opera, reached a peak in the early years of the nineteenth, declined steadily, and died out altogether in the early decades of the present century, though some singers still claim to be in touch with the tradition. A study of the development of the operatic orchestra makes it quite clear that singing styles must have changed in the nineteenth century. A singer could no longer sing as he had in the previous century—he simply would not have been heard. Conversely, once singers adjusted their techniques to overcome the competition of the new orchestra, they were no longer equipped to sing in the older style.

The nineteenth-century operatic orchestra was too magnificent an instrument to waste, and not unexpectedly composers began casting around for additional ways to use it. The basso continuo finally disappeared from opera early in the century, and the orchestra took over the job of accompanying recitative. This accompaniment was generally light, furnished by a small group of instruments selected for their appropriate tone color and ability to produce sounds subordinate to those made by the singer. But on occasion, at high dramatic moments, much more of the orchestra was employed.

In earlier operas, the music simply stopped at the end of one scene and began again with the next. Some nineteenth-century composers began linking scenes with orchestral interludes, reflective or dramatic in nature, perhaps serving to establish the mood of the new scene. In such passages the composer could do whatever he wanted to with his orchestra, without worrying about singers.

The orchestra had been used to play melodic lines before, of course, in purely instrumental sections (overtures, dance music) and in preludes, interludes, and postludes to arias or ensembles. But with so many instruments in the pit capable of playing melodic lines with such variety of orchestral color, composers often called on them for this purpose even when there was singing going on. When the orchestra was first used to accompany singers in the eighteenth century, it did just that—with simple chords and figures which were of no melodic interest and would in no way detract from the melodies being sung on stage. But in the nineteenth century the melodic interest of a section of an aria was often in the pit, played by one or more instruments there, while the singer would have some simple recitative-like passage. The example is from Spontini's *La Vestale*.

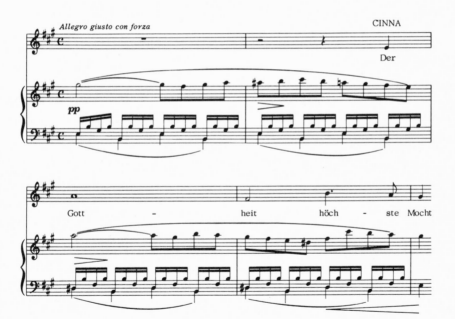

The nineteenth-century orchestra was used to accompany pantomime and gesture, and to take over a certain amount of character portrayal. In the early centuries of opera, the personality and mood of a character was revealed by the libretto, while the orchestra was noncommittal, playing the same sort of music for one character as for another. Not so in the nineteenth century, when composers became fond of using different orchestral sounds for different characters. Hunding in Wagner's *Die Walküre* is introduced by sombre, brusque, militant brass chords that tell us much about the sort of person he is before he utters a word. Baron Ochs, in Strauss's *Der Rosenkavalier*, has to contend throughout much of the opera with rather silly waltz-like music which suggests one side of his character. As Otello enters Desdemona's bedroom in the last act of Verdi's opera, the double basses give out a sinister melody in their lowest register, telling us his state of mind and hinting at the melancholy events to follow. Even a cursory search through other operas of the century would turn up dozens of other examples of the use of the orchestra to suggest something about the character and mood of someone on stage. Wagner felt that this was one of the things music could do best: that when a situation dealt with reason, words were the operatic composer's best tool, but that the more a situation shaded into emotion, the more effective music would be.

Before the nineteenth century, each aria or ensemble had its own musical material, which was never used elsewhere in the opera. But composers discovered that striking, easily remembered musical ideas used in a certain situation became associated with this situation in the audience's mind (or ears), and could be used again later in the opera to create such an association. Thus Samiel, the Evil One in *Der Freischütz*, always appears to the accompaniment of the same music, a diminished chord in the strings over a sinister-sounding thudding bass.

As Cho-Cho-San waits for her husband to return to the last act of *Madame Butterfly*, she speaks of his farewell to her, and the orchestra quotes part of the melody to which this farewell was sung. When Mimi is brought in, dying, in the last act of *La Bohème*, the orchestra gives out the most memorable part of her aria from the love scene which had brought the first act to a close, against the recitative-like chatter of the other characters. This also was such a common technique of the century that dozens of other incidents could be cited.

The most systematic and extensive use of recurring thematic material is found in the late works of Richard Wagner, which are built largely on constantly recurring melodic fragments which build up associative values as the operas unfold. A character comes on stage and is introduced with a melodic idea which is repeated and subjected to various transformations. The same material is heard the next time he enters. Perhaps he is not on stage, but his name is mentioned, whereupon the orchestra plays around with his motif. By this time it should be evident to anyone in the audience that this melodic idea is associated with him, that it is his *leitmotif*, and whenever it recurs, it will bring him to mind. Likewise if some obvious emotional state is established and a melodic fragment is played repeatedly, this fragment will carry with it afterwards the association of this emotion. Leitmotifs may be built up for objects (swords and the like) and even abstract concepts. Once such associations have been established, the composer can use them in various ways. Reference can be made to a person or object not on stage. Two motifs can be played against one another, suggesting some relationship between them. The character of a motif can be altered by modulation, reharmonization, or melodic alteration, suggesting some modification of the original association. Wagner's orchestra often tells us things that we would not otherwise know.

THE TWENTIETH CENTURY: REACTION AGAINST THE GIANT ORCHESTRA

The operatic orchestra increased in size and complexity through the seventeenth, eighteenth, and nineteenth centuries, and into the first years of the twentieth. Artists of a given period often rebel with enthusiasm against the practices of a previous age, however, and there has been a reversal of attitude towards the orchestra in the last four or five decades, partly as a reaction against the tenets of the nineteenth century.

Kurt Weill's fantastically successful *Die Dreigroschenoper* (*Three Penny Opera*), first done in Berlin in 1928, used an orchestra as far removed from that of the late nineteenth century as could be imagined.

tenor saxophone (doubling soprano sax, bassoon, clarinet)
alto saxophone (doubling flute, clarinet)

2 trumpets
trombone (doubling string bass)
banjo (doubling cello and guitar)
timpani, drums
harmonium (doubling celesta)
piano

Only nine players are called for, many of them required to switch from one instrument to others in the course of the work. This orchestra is much more in the tradition of theater bands of the time, groups owing something of their makeup and style of playing to American jazz, which was sweeping Europe at this time, than in that of the operatic orchestra. But Benjamin Britten's *Albert Herring* (1947), a work more in the mainstream of traditional operatic practice and regularly done in the professional opera houses of Europe, calls for an orchestra of comparable size.

flute, oboe, clarinet, bassoon
French horn
percussion, harp, piano
string quartet, double bass

Britten wants only 13 players. This orchestra, with several keyboard instruments, a core of string players, and a handful of winds, is comparable in size and makeup to one from the late seventeenth century. And even such a work as Hindemith's *Mathis der Maler* (Zurich, 1938), written for performance by large professional companies, requiring a large cast of good principals and elaborate staging and costuming, in every sense a large-scale work, calls for an orchestra of strings, 8 woodwinds, and 10 brass, more comparable to one of the larger late eighteenth-century orchestras than to the ideal of Wagner and Strauss:

2 flutes, 2 oboes, 2 clarinets, 2 bassoons
4 French horns, 2 trumpets, 3 trombones, tuba
timpani, 2 percussionists
strings

To balance the winds, a string section quite a bit smaller than those of the late nineteenth century is needed. The work sounds best with an orchestra of some 50 players.

There is another reason for the small size of the instrumental group used in many recent operas, a purely practical one. The twentieth century has been marked by alienation of composer and audience. For reasons too complicated to go into at this point, professional opera houses (particularly in this country) have chosen to continue performing works of previous centuries rather than to do new works. Composers who wish to have operas performed have been forced to turn to other sorts of groups: college workshops or amateur community and church groups. These usually have modest resources, vocally and instrumentally, and composers have made the necessary adjustments. Such works, usually modest in length and in the demands made on singers, instrumentalists, and producers, have been called *chamber operas*.

Hugo Weisgall's *The Stronger* is such a work, a one-character opera of modest dimensions, scored for:

alto saxophone (doubling other woodwind instruments)
tenor saxophone (also doubling other instruments)
trumpet
piano
1 violin, 1 viola, 1 cello, 1 bass

Only 8 players are needed; there is no string section, but rather four solo string players. The orchestra is not unlike some of the early seventeenth century, a small collection of solo instruments.

Even though Menotti's *Amahl and the Night Visitors* was first performed on television, it was written for performance by school and other amateur groups, and is in every way a typical chamber opera. Menotti calls for the following players.

flute, 2 oboes, clarinet, bassoon
horn, trumpet
harp, piano, percussion
strings

Menotti does not specify the number of strings, which may vary from performance to performance. But even though the full string sections of school and community orchestras have on occasion been used, the work sounds best with a total orchestra of no more than 25 players —curiously enough, the size of Mozart's orchestra.

Small as these orchestras are, it is not always possible for amateur groups to find or afford even these players. Chamber operas are often done with nothing more than two pianos, a piano and an organ, or

A contemporary chamber opera, The Widow, by the young American composer Kenneth Gaburo, as performed by the University of Illinois Opera Workshop.

even a single piano, furnishing the accompaniment. This is an absolute reversal of the nineteenth-century ideal. Singers find themselves doing just what performers in the very first operas did: singing to the accompaniment of a single chord-playing instrument.

Whether they are writing for small or large forces, twentieth-century composers favor a sound concept quite different from the massed, thick, homogeneous orchestral sound of the previous century: a clean, transparent, highly variable, constantly shifting palette of instrumental color. Contemporary composers sometimes use a sizable orchestra for their operas; Hans Werner Henze's orchestra for his *Elegy for Young Lovers* (1961) seems to be a near relative of those of the late nineteenth century, in the number of different instruments.

flute, English horn, clarinet
alto saxophone, bassoon
horn, trumpet, trombone
timpani, glockenspiel, celesta
musical saw
marimbaphone, vibraphone
mandolin, guitar
harp, piano
battery I (3 tom-toms, 2 snare drums, woodblock, metal
    blocks)
battery II (3 *crotali*, 3 suspended cymbals, 3 triangles, 3
    bells)
battery III (3 tamtams, bass drum, *maracas*, 3 *tamburi*
    baschi, 3 bongos, 6 tubular bells)
2 violins
viola, cello, bass

This is an orchestra of incredible richness and variety, but in structure and use it has almost nothing to do with a nineteenth-century one. There are only 26 players, and in the course of the opera only a handful of them play at any given moment, with rare exceptions. The sound is almost always light, delicate, transparent; it almost never competes with the sound of the voices; the singers rarely find it necessary to strain or force their voices to be heard over the orchestral sound. The effect is somewhat similar to that in early seventeenth-century operas, in which a rich variety of instruments was assembled, but only a few appropriate ones were used at a time.

In past centuries, opera has often been in the van of musical innovation. Many composers who were trying out and accepting new concepts, who were thought of as "radicals" by their more cautious contemporaries, found opera an excellent place for experimentation and development of new ideas. Putting it more strongly, from the early seventeenth century through the end of the nineteenth, from Monteverdi through Wagner, Strauss, and Debussy, most of the more progressive composers, the men who were expanding the boundaries of musical style, were concerned with opera. There is a simple explanation for this. Audiences traditionally react against innovation and cling to familiar concepts until composers push them to an acceptance of new ones. In opera, with music usually relating to a dramatic situation, audiences are more willing to accept unfamiliar sounds as part of the total happening than they would be if the same sounds were offered them in concert. This phenomenon is readily observed in our contemporary culture, in a slightly different guise: many people accept types of music as background to movies and television plays that would upset them in a recital or concert. But with a few notable exceptions, the most widely performed twentieth-century operas are in conservative styles. The most important musical innovation of the century has taken place outside of the opera house. For the last decade or so, many of our best composers have been involved in experimentation with sound, in the synthesis of sound, in various aspects of electronic music, in testing effects of chance and random composition, in working with various sorts of improvisatory practices. Not much of this has showed up yet in opera, although recent works by the Swedish composer Blomdahl (*Aniara*) and the Italian Luigi Nono (*Intolleranza 1963*) have made use of electronic music. It seems safe to predict that more of the new concepts of sound will be used in opera—and that when this is done by first-rate composers, audience reaction may be much more favorable.

ON- AND OFFSTAGE MUSIC

In all periods some composers have not been satisfied to fill the orchestra pit with players, but have scattered more instruments around the stage as well. This is often done in collaboration with the librettist, who writes a scene which somehow involves onstage instruments.

During a gladiatorial contest in the first act of Cavalli's *Scipione Africano* (Venice, 1664), the pit orchestra stops while a group of onstage musicians, part of the crowd assembled to watch the spectacle, plays. In the third act of Handel's *Almira*, musicians process across the stage playing oboes, trumpets, cymbals, flutes, drums, a hurdy-gurdy, and a bagpipe. These are naturalistic scenes, with the musicians part of the stage spectacle.

The set of the third act of Samuel Barber's *Vanessa* depicts the entrance hall of a country estate; it is New Year's Eve, and a dance is in progress in the ballroom, which can be seen through the open French doors. Groups of dancers can be seen, and an orchestra, which from time to time can be heard playing by itself or with the pit orchestra. There is a similar scene in the third act of Britten's *Peter Grimes*: the action takes place in a street outside the Moot Hall, in which a "barn dance" is taking place. The band—2 clarinets, a violin, a double bass, and a drum—can be heard now and then. And the last scene of the first act of Mozart's *Don Giovanni* has not one, but three, onstage bands playing simultaneously. The scene is set at a ball, and soon an orchestra of 2 oboes, 2 horns, and strings strikes up a minuet. Soon another stage band (violin and basso continuo) starts a second dance, then a third (also violin and continuo) still another dance. The three groups play for awhile, three different dances in different meters.

Sometimes only a single onstage instrument is called for. The nightwatchman in Wagner's *Die Meistersinger* blows his horn at the end of the second act, intoning a single note (F$\sharp$) to signal that the villagers must quiet down and get off the streets. A different sort of problem is posed in Britten's *Turn of the Screw*, in which Miles, one of the children, is asked to accompany an entire scene by playing a piano on stage. The demands for this role are extraordinary, incidentally: it must be sung by a young boy with an unbroken voice who can master the quite complex score, sing his part against the orchestra, and also play a difficult piano part. Hugo Weisgall's *Six Characters in Search of an Author*, based on the play by Pirandello, also uses an onstage piano, played by the "accompanist," sometimes sounding alone and sometimes with the pit orchestra.

For the Paris performance of his *Macbeth*, Verdi called for extra instrumental forces, not on the stage but under it. Two oboes, 6 clarinets, 1 bassoon, and a contrabassoon, invisible to the audience, accompany the scene of the apparition of the eight kings.

No composer has made as extensive use of additional instrumental forces as Wagner. His early opera *Rienzi* uses a stage band of 6 trumpets, 6 natural trumpets, 6 trombones, 4 ophicleides, 8 drums, bells, tamtam, and organ. *Tannhäuser* has stage music in almost every scene. In the opening sequence in Venusberg, a band of 2 each of flutes, clarinets, horns, and bassoons in the left wing of the stage is answered by a similar group in the right wing. An English horn is needed in the next scene, and a bit later a group of pilgrims is heralded by 12 French horns. The Procession of the Guests in the second act takes place to the sound of a dozen onstage trumpets. And at the musical climax of the third act, the pit orchestra is augmented by a wind band (1 piccolo, 2 flutes, 2 oboes, 3 clarinets, 2 horns, 2 bassoons, a percussion) in the wings to right and left. The audience is attacked with sound from three sides in a remarkable anticipation of stereophonic sound.

Stage music, and offstage music, have attracted composers from the early days of opera to the present by their potentialities for added sound, color, and spectacle.

SUMMARY

For the first century or so of opera, composers accompanied their solo singers lightly, with a basso continuo of a chord-playing instrument supported by a stringed bass instrument. Other instruments, often in rich variety, played only in purely instrumental sections or to accompany a chorus. By the first half of the eighteenth century, more instruments were used to accompany arias, but composers treated them in antiphonal fashion with the voice or had them play light sustaining chords or simple accompanimental patterns. A favorite device was to have a solo instrument or two treated in obbligato style to the voice, both accompanied by the continuo.

Later in the eighteenth century the operatic orchestra was standardized into a basic string choir augmented by a small number of winds and sometimes a percussion instrument or two. The string choir took over the job of accompanying singers, though at first it was treated very much the same as a continuo, playing simple chords and accompanimental figures which in no way threatened the supremacy of the voice. But as the orchestra increased in size and complexity in the nineteenth century, composers made more and more use of it and often required their singers to sing against a full orchestra of as many as a hundred instruments. This huge orchestra took on new jobs (accompanying recitative, accompanying gesture, pantomime, and other stage action) and even took over some tasks formerly assigned only to the singers.

The present century has seen a reaction against the mammoth orchestra, with composers (from choice or necessity) writing for much smaller groups, and preferring a thinner, more varied sound than was favored in the past century.

VIII

PRELUDE AND OVERTURE

In almost every opera ever written, the orchestra has some preliminary music before the singers apear on stage and the action gets
under way. This is one of the occasions where the composer is free
to use his orchestra in any way he desires, without concern for balance
between it and the voice and without a text to impose its own form
on the music. Some composers have taken this opportunity to write
ambitious orchestral works which may or may not have anything to
do with the opera which is to follow; others have used it for completely different purposes. Often the nature of this preliminary music
gives a strong clue as to what sort of work the composer has written,
how closely the various elements of the work will be integrated, and
what attitude the composer has taken on the most fundamental matter
in all opera, the relative importance given to words and to music.

THE CALL TO ATTENTION

Igor Stravinsky's *The Rake's Progress* (1948–1951), the
most ambitious of his operas, commences with a vigorous "Prelude,"
19 measures of a loud brass fanfare mostly on the dominant and tonic
chords of E major. This music is separated from the beginning of
the first scene by a pause, during which the curtain is opened.
Musically, it has no connection whatsoever with anything that happens
later; it is in a different key, tempo, dynamic level, and mood from
the music of the first scene. Its function is simply to announce that
the opera is beginning, to alert the audience that they should take

their seats, if they are not already there, quiet down, and begin paying attention to the stage. It is too brief to have more than a rudimentary formal construction or to be of any musical interest in itself, lasting barely half a minute. Its purpose is functional—to announce the beginning of the opera—and it does this in a straightforward, direct way, with no lingering over unnecessary details.

The use of preliminary music for such a purpose is by no means original with Stravinsky. The first full-length opera, Monteverdi's *Orfeo* of 1607, starts with a strikingly similar call to attention. It also is scored for brass, consists almost entirely of dominant and tonic fanfare figures, and has no musical relationship to anything that happens in the opera. It is also a functional prelude, and it performs its function crisply and impressively.

The use of a bit of music as a rhetorical beginning, as a sort of gesture to announce that the evening's entertainment is commencing, is pared down to its epitome by Virgil Thomson in his setting of Gertrude Stein's *The Mother of Us All*. There is a snare drum roll, then come five loud staccato major triads, and the opera gets under way.

None of these compositions is extended enough, or interesting enough musically, to make any sense divorced from the opera it serves. Even though none has any musical or emotive connection with the opera which follows, each is dependent on it for its existence and would have no life of its own if separated from it.

PRELUDE

Many art songs begin with a prelude for the accompanying piano which serves to establish the key in which the song begins, to set the meter, and perhaps to sketch in the mood of the beginning lines. Such a prelude may be a phrase or two in length, coming to a cadence before the entrance of the voice, or it may last for only a few measures and lead directly into the vocal line without pause. Schubert's *Das Wandern* has such a prelude: 3½ measures setting the key, mood, and tempo before the voice enters (shown opposite).

Preliminary music in an opera may serve the same purpose. For example, the 19 measures of somber orchestral music which sound before the curtain in Debussy's *Pelléas et Mélisande* prepare us for the physical setting, the dense, thick, dark forest in which Golaud is lost, and for the gloomy mood with which the opera begins. Verdi's *Il Trovatore* starts off with a brief prelude based on a drum roll, arpeggios in the strings, and a horn call, musical material which is

Mässig geschwind

Wan - dern ist des Mül - lers— Lust, das Wan - dern!

continued into the first scene. Britten, in his *Peter Grimes,* has his orchestra give out no more than 4 measures, based on a figure derived from the spoken rhythm of the name "Peter Grimes," before the singing starts.[1]

Moderato ma energico

HOBSON

Pe - ter Grimes!

[1] Copyright 1945 by Boosey & Hawkes, Ltd. Reprinted by permission.

Strauss's *Elektra* starts with a mere 4 measures of rhythmic treatment of the *d* minor triad before the first singer begins; the effect is very much the same as an accompanist striking a few chords to give a singer the pitch. The same composer's *Salome* has only 3 measures of prelude before Narraboth's famous first line, "*Wie schön ist die Prinzessin Salome heute Nacht*"; Milhaud's *David*, a work of mammoth proportions, has 3 measures in the orchestra before the opening chorus of Israelites; Berg allows 3 measures for the opening of the first curtain in *Wozzeck* before the first singer (singing a D and C against the D♭ given by the orchestra); and Schoenberg allows 3 measures for the curtain, and for the single character to make her entrance and convey to the audience the impression that she is lost, is his *Erwartung*. Brief as these may be, they still perform the function of key- and mood-setting preludes satisfactorily.

While many composers have used preliminary music only for the first act and have begun later acts immediately with an aria, chorus, ensemble, or even recitative, others have preferred to articulate the opening of later acts with preludes also. For instance, the second act of Verdi's *A Masked Ball* begins with a *scena*, a rather elaborate recitative and aria, for Adelisa, but this is preceded by stormy music from the orchestra,

which is replaced by a more expressive theme as she appears. This prelude goes on for some hundred measures, then comes to a pause before her first line of recitative. This is a more elaborate prelude than Verdi would have written had the scene occurred somewhere in the middle of an act. And Wagner, a master of this sort of thing, begins the second act of *Lohengrin* with gloomy music in the lower strings and later winds, as we see Ortrud and Frederick brooding outside the fortress of Antwerp. There is an interruption of festive music sounding from inside the palace (played by an onstage wind band), then silence and resumption of the first material before the dialogue begins. This is first-rate tone painting, establishing the mood (and key) in which the act begins.

Such preludes, whether they open an opera or are used for later acts, are merely preparation for what is to follow and, like the call-to-attention prelude, are almost never substantial enough in musical content to make any sense by themselves. They also are functional, though their function is different from the preludes of the first type discussed earlier.

THE POTPOURRI OPENING

Benjamin Britten's version of the popular eighteenth-century *Beggars' Opera* begins with a beggar appearing before the curtain and addressing the audience. The orchestra begins to tune up, and he breaks off with "Come! Play away the overture!" as the curtain rises. During this overture, each of the leading characters appears on stage and is seen in some characteristic pose or activity while the orchestra plays one of the tunes which he will sing later in the opera. Lucy Lockit is seen first, and the orchestra plays "Come Sweet Lass," which she sings in the third act. Polly Peachum is introduced by "Virgins Are Like the Fair Flowers," Mrs. Trapes by "In the Days of my Youth," and Mr. Lockit by "Thus Gamesters United." The "hero," Captain Macheath, is greeted by a simple variation on his first song, "My Heart Was so Free," Mrs. Peachum by "If Any Wench Venus's Girdle Wear," and the Gentlemen of the Road by "Fill Ev'ry Glass." Next the Ladies of the Town enter, to "Gamesters and Lawyers Are Jugglers Alike," and finally we see Mr. Peachum, while the orchestra plays a version of "Through All the Employments of Life," the tune with which he begins the first act.

Though Britten calls this an overture, it consists merely of some of the tunes from the opera strung together, in various keys, each of them stated in a rather simple form and none of them subjected to musical development. It could conceivably be played as an orchestral work, separated from the opera, but it would be rather unsatisfactory this way. It has no particular key scheme, no formal organization beyond the mere succession of simple tunes. The term *potpourri* was used in the nineteenth century for a type of salon music, usually for piano and designed for musical amateurs, made up of a succession of well-known tunes strung together, and the term has been taken over for an overture of this sort. A potpourri proper was designed for consumption by less-than-professional musicians, who would respond better to such a simple musical event than to a more sophisticated, formally complex type of "art" music; operatic overtures built in this way have proved to be likewise easily comprehended, and many of the more popular operas of the past century begin with this sort of preliminary music.

Bizet's *Carmen*, for instance, starts off with several tunes which are to figure prominently in the course of the opera. First we hear the lively music which will be heard at the beginning of the bullfight scene, then the melody of Escamillo's "Toreador" song; after a return to the bullfight music, the harmonic and melodic motive which will be associated with "fate" leads to a pause before the first scene commences. This serves admirably as a beginning for *Carmen*: it establishes several of the moods which are to dominate; it introduces (or reintroduces) the audience to some of the most important melodic material; it is lively and loud enough also to function as a call to attention. But it would make no sense played by itself, divorced from the opera. The melodies are offered briefly, then dropped without any sort of development. It is too brief, too much a patchwork of short ideas, to be a satisfactory piece of music.

Bizet calls this a prelude, not an overture. Composers are by no means consistent in their terminology, and it might be wise for us to continue using the term *prelude* for any preliminary music which is dependent on the following opera for its existence, which is not substantial enough musically to stand alone; and to reserve the term *overture* for a composition which is extended and coherent enough to make musical sense if detached.

Ambroise Thomas's *Mignon* begins with another potpourri. After a few preliminary *andantino* measures, setting the key and settling the audience, a section with harp arpeggios, *moderato sostenuto*, anticipates the first entrance of Lothario, the aged harper.

A change of meter brings the melody of Mignon's *"Connais-tu le pays,"* which she will sing at the end of the first act.

Now, in another key and in a different tempo, Thomas introduces the melody of Philina's brilliant Polonaise from the second act, *"Je suis Titania."*

This is treated in rather extended fashion, bringing the "Overture," as he calls it, to a rousing close. This is a much longer piece than the *Carmen* prelude, and is completely separated from the beginning of the first act, but it is still nothing more than a string of melodies taken from the opera, and the fact that Thomas begins it in the key of A♭ and ends in the key of A is a clue that he did not consider it a self-contained composition.

A lively rhythmic figure, *vivace,* begins the "Prologue" to Leon-cavallo's *I Pagliacci* and is used later to give some semblance of coherence to its rambling structure. The music soon slows down to *largo assai* for the most notorious tune of the opera, the *"Ridi,*

Pagliaccio" section of Canio's *"Vesti la giubba"* aria from the end of the first act. Next we hear some of the love music sung by Nedda and Silva in the third scene of the first act, *"Si, t'amo! t'amo!"* A brief return to the original *vivace* material leads to something unexpected: Tonio, one of the characters, looks through the curtains, then comes forward and sings at some length, explaining that what is to happen on the stage should not be regarded as make-believe, but rather as "a bit of life true to nature." As he retires, a few measures of the original *vivace* music lead to the first curtain and give a faint suggestion of formal coherence, though not enough to suggest that the prologue should be performed alone.

Such preliminary music has also been used in the twentieth century. Carlisle Floyd's *Susannah*, one of the most widely performed American operas of a few years ago, starts off with some "Opening Music," as he calls it, consisting of a succession of chord patterns associated with a scene of the Elders, some music which later serves as the accompaniment to a duet by Susannah and Little Bat in the fifth scene ("You didn't! You didn't! You couldn't have! It's a lie!"), and finally some of the "Ain't it a pretty night?" music from the second scene. This opening music gives a preview of what lies in store for the audience; there would seem to be no reason to play it by itself.

Sometimes only one or two of the musical ideas to be heard later in the opera will serve as a prelude. For instance, Verdi's *Traviata* opens with a prelude based on two motives from the opera, the first a sweet, sentimental, chromatically harmonized fragment associated with Violetta's illness, and the second a more extended treatment of a melody which she will sing in the second act, *"Amami, Alfredo, amami quant'io t'amo."* This is not a prelude offering material from the first scene, leading directly into it, of the type discussed earlier. There is a complete break before the first scene, which then begins with completely different material and mood. Nevertheless, though only two melodies are presented, they are ones which will occur later in the opera, and in intent and effect the prelude is similar to the more extended potpourri beginnings discussed above.

The same composer's *Rigoletto* starts with a prelude based on one of the most prominent motives from the opera, later associated with Rigoletto's curse on his tormenters. After 34 measures of development of this one idea, *andante sostenuto*, the curtain opens and the first scene starts off with altogether different music. Puccini's *Tosca* has a mere 3 measures of introductory music, a simple statement of a motive later associated with the villain Scarpia, before the first scene begins. Of course these are far too brief to have any musical significance apart from the operas they serve to introduce. In a way, they function as a call to attention and are similar to some of the quite brief sections discussed above. But there is a difference, in that they also introduce the listener to some significant musical material which will be heard later. Nor are they preludes to first scenes, since the motives they offer are from later in the opera.

THE FORMALIZED OVERTURE

Pergolesi's setting of *Il Prigioniero Superbo* (1733) has an "Introduzione" beginning with fanfare-like figures in the key of D, mostly on the tonic and dominant chords.

This is quite similar to the call-to-attention preludes of the Stravinsky and Monteverdi operas mentioned in the first section of this chapter. But here the music begins to take its own course. After 38 measures of development of this material, a change of key (from D major to *d* minor) and of tempo (from *allegro* to *largo*) brings a contrasting melodic motive.

After brief treatment of this motive, there is a return to the original key and tempo, and 56 measures in triple meter bring the overture to an end.

The three short sections are complete in themselves; though each is too brief to stand alone, the three together make a more extended piece with a satisfactory key scheme (D—*d*—D) and a simple but effective formal scheme—ABA. None of the melodic material is drawn from the opera, and the piece makes sense itself as a piece of music. It could conceivably be part of an orchestral program.

This, then, is a somewhat different concept of the orchestral beginning for an opera. The piece serves the function of announcing the commencement of the opera, but in addition it is a more complex and complete musical composition than those discussed to this point, and is in no way dependent on the following opera. Despite Pergolesi's title for the piece, it can be classified as an overture, this term denoting preliminary music which is written in some complete and satisfactory musical form.

Overtures with such a fast—slow—fast structure came to be known as Italian overtures. Another example opens Jean-Jacques Rousseau's *Le Devin du Village*. (Although this opera is in French, written by a Frenchman, it is not surprising to find that it has an Italian overture: Rousseau felt that the "ills" of French opera could be cured by the introduction of many stylistic elements of Italian opera.) With its D major—*d* minor—D major key scheme and its *gai*—*lent*—*gai* tempo pattern, it is a very near relative to Pergolesi's overture. Since each is a formalized musical structure, unrelated in mood and melodic material to the opera which it serves to introduce, no damage would be done by interchanging the two: Pergolesi's overture would serve Rousseau's opera satisfactorily, and vice versa, even though one is a tragedy and the other a comedy.

Another stylized form is the French overture, a well-known example of which begins Purcell's *Dido and Aeneas*. The beginning is slow, an *adagio* with sustained chords. After some development of this material, there is a change to a fast tempo *(allegro)* and a contrast of texture: a lively arpeggio pattern is treated in imitation, each of the strings having it in turn. At the end there is a broadening of tempo, suggesting a return to the slow beginning.

The characteristic form of the French overture (slow, homophonic—fast, imitative—hint of return to slow) can be followed in the overture to a most familiar work, Handel's *Messiah*. A more recent example is the overture to Kurt Weill's *Die Dreigroschenoper;* even though there is no tempo change, the overture clearly divides into an opening homophonic section, a contrasting imitative one, and a return to the homophonic opening.

The French and Italian overtures owe nothing to opera for their characteristic form and musical styles. They are instrumental works which follow forms and styles and musical procedures of other

Siegmund and Sieglinde in the first act of Wagner's Die Walküre. Bayreuth, 1963.

The prologue to the eighteenth-century French opera, Hippolyte et Aricie,
by Jean-Phillippe Rameau, as produced in 1966 by
The Opera Company of Boston.

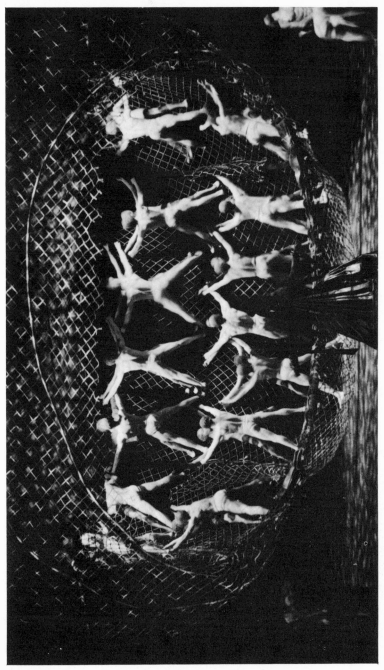

The Venusberg scene in the first act of Wagner's Tannhäuser, as staged at Bayreuth in 1962 by Wieland Wagner.

The Opera Company of Boston

The death of the Commandante in the first act of Mozart's
Don Giovanni, as presented by The Opera
Company of Boston.

instrumental works of the time, and they are by no means used only in opera. Oratorios, other dramatic works, and ballets may begin with such overtures, identical in style and form to those found in operas. They may serve as the first section of a group of purely instrumental works, they may appear in keyboard compositions, or they may be independent instrumental works, not intended to introduce anything.

When an overture is conceived as a formalized instrumental work, owing nothing to the opera which follows, it is tied to it by nothing more than association. It would seem wrong to us to have another overture at the beginning of the *Messiah*, but there are many overtures to Handel's operas which would have served just as well, and we could just as easily come to associate one of these with the oratorio and feel that *it* was the proper one. There are many instances of composers themselves using the same formalized overture for different works, or different overtures for the same work.

A classic case involves the overture which now serves Rossini's *Barber of Seville*. In Rossini's time the most widely used formal construction for an extended movement or an isolated piece was what is now called sonata-allegro form. A slow introduction was optional; the body of the piece, in a faster tempo usually, would begin with a clearly defined theme in the tonic key; a modulation to a closely related key (dominant, or relative major if the first theme had been in minor) would lead to a new theme, followed often by a third theme also in this new key; then one or more of the main themes would be subjected to various types of treatment in different keys, in a section called the development; finally there would be a recapitulation, with all themes repeated in the tonic key, and possibly a coda, a final rounding off.

The overture to *The Barber* begins with a slow section, *andante maestoso*, in which several fragments of melodic material are introduced and toyed with briefly. The main theme is given out in the key of *e* minor at the beginning of the main, *allegro* section of the overture.

After a modulation to G major, the second, contrasting theme comes in.

The development section is almost completely done away with, a concession to the fact that this is after all an operatic overture and not a symphonic movement. After only a few measures, the first and then the second main themes return, both now in the tonic. A spirited coda, in E major, brings the overture to a rousing conclusion.

The overture serves perfectly as an introduction to this opera. The slow section prepares the audience for the lyric, sentimental scenes, the *allegro* sets a lively, *buffo* atmosphere which will prevail for the bulk of the opera. There is no thematic relationship between overture and opera—for good reason. Rossini first used it for his opera *L'Equivoco Stravagante* in 1811, then for *Auerliano in Palmira* in 1814, and again in 1815 for *Elisabetta, Regina d'Inghilterra*. It satisfied him equally as an overture for the serious *Elisabetta* and the comic *Barber*.

The overture to Paul Hindemith's *Mathis der Maler* is a complete symphonic composition, which is worked out in just the ways we find in his instrumental works. This "Vorspiel" has been a successful concert piece, as the first section of the symphonic suite *Mathis der Maler*, which was put together from three sections of the opera.

But some composers have not been content to have such a complete break between a formalized overture and the opera it serves to introduce. Gluck says in the preface to his opera *Alceste*, "I feel that the overture should inform the audience of the nature of the action which is to follow and in a way to present the argument of what is to come." The overture to *Alceste* is a rather long, intricate orchestral piece. A somber motive is stated first in *d* minor, followed by a slightly faster, plaintive figure in the strings.

A modulatory section leads to a *fortissimo* statement of a second motive, in full orchestra.

There is finally a shorter third theme, stated for the most part over a prolonged pedal point on A.

Now the three sections are stated again, in a sort of recapitulation but in different keys: the first in *a* minor, the second in F major, and the last in *d* minor. The overture does not come to a conclusion: the last motive is extended, over a dominant pedal point, to lead directly into the opening chorus of the first act.

Supplied with a suitable ending, the overture would be usable as a concert piece. It is strong enough, formally, to stand by itself. But it makes more sense in the setting in which the composer conceived of it, as the first section of a dramatic work. Its somber, slow-moving chords, the alternations between loud outbursts from the entire orchestra and quieter, more gentle figurations in the strings or winds establish an exalted mood of tragedy—or, rather, preparation for tragedy. Somehow, the feeling is anticipatory. The effect is that something is about to happen: an opera. And not just any opera, but this specific one. The overture would not work well for any of Gluck's other operas. It belongs with *Alceste*, not because of thematic identity, but because it establishes the proper mood.

Mozart's overture to *Figaro* is a similar instance of an overture fitting a specific opera. It also is a complete piece, in sonata-allegro form, and is frequently and successfully performed on orchestral programs, completely divorced from its parent opera. But Mozart wrote it specifically to go with *Figaro*, and even though none of the melodic material of the overture shows up in the course of the opera, the whole mood and movement of the piece sets the perfect tone for the bustling, sophisticated comedy which is to follow. Other Mozart overtures are in precisely the same form, but it would not work to use the *Figaro* overture as preparation for a performance of *Don Giovanni*, or to use the *Magic Flute* overture to lead into the first act of *Figaro*. The distinction between these overtures and the purely formalized ones discussed earlier is a subtle, but nevertheless real, one. Overtures like those to *Dido and Aeneas*, *Le Devin du Village*, and *The Barber of Seville* are abstract and formalized; the Mozart and Gluck overtures are for specific operas.

A more recent example of an overture which is musically complete, which has no specific musical relationship to its opera, but which belongs to it in spirit, is that of Menotti's *The Telephone*. Brief though it is, the ABA pattern (*allegro vivace—andantino—allegro vivace*) is perfectly satisfactory, and it could be an attractive, if slight, concert piece. None of the thematic material is drawn from the opera itself, but its disarming triviality and sentimentality puts the audience in the right frame of mind for what is to happen. It would be unthinkable as an introduction to the same composer's *The Medium*, or *The Consul*—or even to *Amahl and the Night Visitors*, which has its own brand of sentimentality.

Mozart's overture to *Don Giovanni* seems to belong in the same class. It is a complete musical work itself (in sonata-allegro form), yet it does an admirable job of setting the stage for this particular opera. There is an even more intimate connection, though: Mozart uses, in the brief slow introduction, a characteristic sequence of chords which will reappear later in the opera, in the climactic scene in which the ghost of the Commandant, whom Don Giovanni kills in the first scene, appears at the Don's banquet and drags him down to his reward.

This overture, then, represents a synthesis of several of the types previously discussed. There is quotation of musical material from the opera itself, but not merely in preludial fashion leading directly into the first scene, nor as a loosely strung together succession of tunes, as in the potpourri opening, but worked into a composition which makes perfect musical sense.

Overtures written in the same form may serve quite different functions. We have seen an overture in sonata-allegro form intended as a formalized opening (*The Barber of Seville*), another one in the same form setting the mood for the specific opera which will follow (*The Marriage of Figaro*), and still another which makes use of a bit of thematic material from its opera. The overture to Weber's *Der Freischütz* represents a further development of this last idea:

it is also in sonata-allegro form, but almost all of its melodic material is drawn from the opera.

There is a brief slow introduction, *adagio;* after a few preliminary measures establishing the key of C major, the French horns give out a lyric, pastoral melody,

which is soon interrupted by the sinister diminished seventh chords which characterize Zamiel, the Black Huntsman.

The exposition begins in *c* minor, *molto vivace,* with the accompaniment and later the melody of the second part of Max's first-act aria *"Durch die Wälder."* The bridge section to the second theme draws on the music of the famous incantation scene in the Wolf's Glen in the second act, the music which accompanies the stage directions "total darkness obscures the sky. Storm of thunder, lightning, and hail; flames start from the earth." That leads to the second theme, in the expected key of E♭ major, a contrasting sustained

melody given out by the clarinet, derived from the very end of *"Durch die Wälder."* The spirited final section of Agatha's *"Leise, leise"* aria serves as a closing theme to the exposition.

The development section begins with the storm music from the Wolf's Glen scene, which shifts to various keys, leads to brief treatment of a fragment from Agatha's aria, and soon arrives at the beginning of the recapitulation. The same themes are repeated, as usual, though the second theme is distorted and mixed up with Zamiel's motive. A vigorous coda, in C major, brings this justly celebrated piece to a fine conclusion.

Drawing all of its melodic material from the opera as it does, this overture has an obvious kinship with the potpourri. But here the tunes are not strung one after another, loosely, but worked into a completely satisfying composition. It has been a popular concert piece for over a hundred years, but it is also a first-rate overture to the opera when it is performed.

⚜ MISCELLANEOUS OPENINGS

Alban Berg's *Lulu* has 6 measures of introductory music which might well serve as a model for "overtures" to operas constructed on serial technique. The essence of this compositional technique is that one or more basic "rows," or "sets," or "cells," are subjected to various permutations—inversions, retrograde treatments, and the like. The material presented in the first 6 measures of *Lulu* is used throughout the opera; in a curious way, this is something like a potpourri opening, offering some of the important musical material from the opera.

Menotti's *The Consul* has no preliminary music from the orchestra. Instead, the first music comes from an offstage phonograph recording of a pseudo-popular song, written by Menotti himself. It is only when Magda slams the window shut that the orchestra takes over its accustomed role.

In Stravinsky's *Oedipus Rex*, the singers begin immediately with the orchestra, on the first chord. And in Carl Orff's version of this same tale, *Oedipus der Tyrann*, the first singer must have his pitch before the curtain opens, since he begins his opening lines before the orchestra is heard.

SUMMARY

Preliminary music from the orchestra may serve many purposes. It may simply announce that something is about to happen. It may serve as a prelude to the first scene, giving out accompaniments or melodies which lead directly to the first vocal entrance. It may prepare the audience for what is to come by offering a succession of prominent melodies from the opera. It may be a carefully constructed composition in its own right, furnishing music for the enjoyment of the audience before the opera proper begins. It may establish a dominant mood of the opera. Or it may combine several of these functions.

IX

DANCE AND PANTOMIME

Any discussion of dance in opera must of necessity proceed along national lines. The French, from the beginning, insisted on dance in their operas; of the operas in the repertory today, it is those by French composers which invariably have dance sequences.

Historically, France was the second country in which opera took root. As might be expected, it was cultivated at the royal court, where it had been preceded by a string of rather loosely constructed musico-dramatic works beginning with the *Ballet comique de la royne* of 1581 and proceeding through a series of pastorales, ballets, and comédies-ballets. Dance was traditionally a favorite pastime of the royalty and nobility, and all of these entertainments were heavily overlaid with dance sequences, sometimes for professionals, sometimes for members of the court.

When the new Italian form of opera was brought to France for the first time in 1645, the court was most pleased with the dance sequences which had been added to make it more palatable to the French taste. Jean-Baptiste Lully, who had been brought to France as a child, from Italy, and had been steadily working his way to a position of prominence in the musical world of his new country, undertook a painstaking study of the inflection of the French language to see how it could most effectively be set to music. He also understood the French fondness for dance, and for classical, dignified, restrained drama. When after a series of crafty manipulations he found himself with a virtual monopoly on the composition and production of opera in France, he was ready with a good librettist (Quinault) to supply him with dramas very much to the taste of his audience, with the technique to set these texts in a way suitable to the French language—and with the understanding that his works should be full of dance. The resulting operas were so well written and so cleverly gauged to French tastes and prejudice that they became a model for most French opera for the next century.

Lully's *Thésée* is typical in its numerous and varied dances. After the overture, there is a lengthy allegorical prologue involving five gods and several choruses, concluding with a lively dance in triple meter; an "air" by Ceres in a contrasting meter, with dancing taking place while he sings; and a second instrumental dance in a slower triple meter. The first act unfolds with recitative, airs, and choruses until the final "sacrifice" scene, which is made up of a march for the entrance of the combatants, a dance sequence for them in a lively duple meter, a fast choral dance in triple time, and a repeat of the march. The dancing in the second act occurs with the entrance of Thésée, carried by four slaves. The third act has a choral dance by the inhabitants of the underworld, the fourth act a dance by those of the Enchanted Island, and the fifth act ends with a *pas de deux* and two dances in contrasting meter. In addition, many of the solo and choral sections are written in dance forms and rhythms, and it was customary to interpolate other, currently popular dances, particularly at the end of the last act. Typical of this era of French opera is the inclusion of dance in every act and the use of sequences of dances in contrasting meters.

Jean-Phillipe Rameau was Lully's most illustrious successor, the first French composer after him whose operas were thought to approach those of Lully. There were, of course, stylistic differences between the two men, but the concept of opera was the same: a succession of episodes, with a more fluent mingling of recitative, air, chorus, and dance than was found in contemporary Italian works. The structure of the third act of his *Dardanus* (1739) is typical:

Scene I	instrumental prelude
	air: Iphise (*"O jour affreux!"*)
Scene II	recitative: Iphise, Antenor
	air: Antenor (*"Quel jour conviendrait"*)
Scene III	choral dance (*"Que l'on chanté"*)
	air gai en rondeau (dance)
	duet: two Phrygians (*"Paix favorable"*)
	menuet (dance)
	menuet en rondeau (dance)
	air: a Phrygian (*"Volez plaisirs"*)

	tambourin (dance)
	second tambourin (dance)
Scene IV	air: Teucer (*"Cessez vos jeux"*)
	chorus (*"Allez et remportez"*)

The dancing is concentrated in the third scene, which is actually a divertissement: the development of the plot stops, though several of the pieces have text, and all attention centers on a succession of dances, in varied meters and tempi. Action resumes only with the entrance of Teucer at the beginning of the following scene.

NINETEENTH-CENTURY STRUGGLES

French opera underwent many changes in the late eighteenth and early nineteenth centuries. As one could guess from the changing patterns of French society and culture during this critical period, opera became no longer the amusement of the aristocracy, but rather an entertainment accessible to a wider cross section of the populace. High-flown, stylized tragedy gave way to more earthy drama. Gods, goddesses, and great historical figures were replaced on the stage by more recognizable human beings, engaged not in the pursuit of lofty aims but in the satisfaction of mere human desires. Some composers attempted to return to some of the notions of earlier aristocratic opera as the nineteenth century unfolded, and French opera developed along two parallel courses for a while, with different opera houses for "comic" and "serious" opera. But a strong common bond between the two was the continuation of the French tradition of dance in opera.

Ballet was worked in most easily in those operas which maintained the closest ties with the earlier operatic tradition. Berlioz's *Les Troyens* has ballet sequences handled very much in the style discussed above. The second act, for example, opens in Dido's gardens by the sea, in Carthage, which are lavishly decorated for the return of Aeneas. After a brief scene of recitative and arioso involving Anna (Dido's sister) and Narbal (Dido's minister), the victorious Aeneas enters, Dido at his side, and is showered with flowers. Dido mounts her throne, with Anna, Aeneas, and Narbal grouped around her, and they—and the audience—watch as Nubian slaves dance a ballet. After this interlude, the opera gets back to business.

This is a typical ballet sequence, in several respects. It is composed of three musical sections, in contrasting meters and tempi.

This contrast is for the benefit of the dancers, to give them the chance to perform several types of dances. Also, different groups of dancers are called for, giving the composer an opportunity to write several sections of different "exotic" music and furnishing the occasion for different costumes. French opera has usually been receptive to spectacle, and any excuse for vivid or unusual costumes is welcome.

The librettists were responsible for bringing about situations on the stage which would allow ballet sequences, and their most common technique was to have them take place during scenes when a number of people were assembled on stage for some sort of ceremony or celebration. This is a dance-within-a-play idea; in order for the audience to observe a ballet, a situation must be brought about on stage which allows dancing, with the participants in the drama making way for the dancers and observing, themselves. For instance, the next-to-last scene in Massenet's pseudo-Biblical *Herodias* takes place in a great hall in Herod's palace. There is a grand procession of some of the principals (Vitellius, Herod, Herodias) and a salutation by the chorus (*"Herode, gloire à toi!"*). Since so many people

have been brought together, it would be a shame for them not to
watch some ballet for a while; so there is a dance of Egyptian women,

then a dance by a group of Babylonian women,

followed by some women of Gaul,

some Phoenician women,

and a final dance by everyone.

After this pleasant diversion for cast and audience, the principals proceed with words and music which carry the drama to its climax.

Saint-Saëns worked with a rather grim story and a tightly organized libretto in his *Samson et Dalila*. There seemed to be little opportunity for dance, but in deference to French taste, a place was found. The first scene of the last act is a bleak one, in which we see Samson imprisoned, blinded, and condemned by his own people for what they take to be his betrayal of them. The following scene takes place in the temple of Dagon, a god of the Philistines. It is daybreak; Dalila and young Philistine women, decked in flowers, enter. A dance of the priestesses is followed by a general bacchanal, naturally with more dancing; the entrance of the blind Samson, led by a child, gets the story back on the track.

Composers and librettists have sometimes gone to considerable pains to find situations which justify the inclusion of ballet. Priestesses of Dagon, or Nubian slaves, or Phoenician women were remote enough from nineteenth-century French audiences so that no shock was occasioned when they broke into dance on the stage; the same was true of ethnic groups engaged in folk ceremonies in operas set in more recent times. But even though opera is built on a series of conventions, it would not have seemed proper for characters in a drama taking place in the present or recent past to have engaged in ballet. Massenet's *Manon* overcomes this problem in ingenious fashion. The third act takes place in Paris, and begins with a crowd scene on the Cours-le-Reine. Guillot de Morfontaine, determined that Manon shall become his mistress, has learned of her interest in opera and ballet—and that her lover, De Bretigny, has not indulged her in this whim. With an air of great importance, Guillot announces to De Bretigny, "The opera, which you have denied her, will soon be here!" then to Manon, "Come, Manon, come over here. The new ballet will be danced for you." The crowd, overhearing this, shouts. At Guillot's signal, the ballet troupe from the Opera House enters and performs, there in the street. Parisians did not engage in dance on the streets of eighteenth-century Paris, but ballet dancers would, if they could somehow be brought there, and Massenet and his librettist manage just this.

At times, ballet in opera is offered openly as diversion, with no attempt to integrate it into the plot. Ambroise Thomas, making an opera of *Hamlet*, was hard pressed to find a suitable place to insert ballet in this gloomy tale. Undaunted, he put it in anyway. The third act ends with an eerie scene between Hamlet and the Queen, in which Hamlet sees and hears the ghost of his father. The fourth-act curtain goes up not on any of the principals, but on the ballet corps, disguised as "Villagers." They dance a *Pas des Chasseurs*, a *Pantomime*, a *Valse-Mazurke*, a *Scene du Bouquet*, a *Polka* of a number of contrasting sections, and a *Strette Finale*. The curtain goes down, the dancers go to their dressing rooms, and now the opera proper resumes with Ophelia's "Mad Scene." No attempt is made to suggest that the ballet has had anything to do with Hamlet.

The French passion for ballet affected composers of other nationalities who wrote or rewrote operas for production in Paris. Rossini was not in the habit of including ballet in his successful Italian operas, but his last opera, *William Tell*, was written expressly for Paris, to a French libretto, and was first performed there in 1829; so it is not surprising to find a *Passo à Sei* in the first act and a lengthy *Ballo di Soldati* in Act III. Both are diversions, interrupting the unfolding of the drama—but they afford the *corps de ballet* the chance to perform. Verdi's *Macbeth* was first done in Florence in 1847, with no sign of ballet. When a Paris performance was proposed, he made some major alterations, one of these being the addition of a ballet scene. As done in France in 1865, it has a ballet sequence at the beginning of the third act, which had originally begun with the famous witches' trio. In a lengthy sequence (*allegro vivacissimo—un poco ritardando—allegro—andante—allegro—valzer —poco più mosso*) the witches dance around a cauldron, summon Hecate, and go through a series of dances with her.

Wagner faced the same problem when *Tannhäuser* was performed in Paris in 1861, and he had even more difficulty in finding a place to insert a ballet. He finally decided to have a dance sequence at the very beginning, in the scene at the court of Venus. In his revision, the first curtain rises on a bacchanal involving nymphs, satyrs, fauns, naiads, cupids, and other kindred spirits. The music is some of the best Wagner ever wrote. But the Parisian audience was not pleased; they not only wanted ballet in their opera, they wanted it in a specific place, later in the work so that they would not miss it if they ate and drank beyond curtain time. Ballet at the beginning of the first act simply would not do, and Wagner's stubbornness on this point had much to do with the unfavorable reception accorded *Tannhäuser*.

🌸 OTHER COUNTRIES

Ballet was not found exclusively in French opera; examples can be found in operas written for various other countries, throughout much of the history of opera. Many of the earliest Italian operas call for some dancing. Peri's *Euridice* closes with a simple dance, and Monteverdi has his shepherds dance in *Orfeo*. Early English opera was influenced by two main forces, the pre-opera Masque (consisting of poetry, song, dance, and sometimes instrumental music, casually strung together) and French opera, in both of which dance played a prominent part. It comes as no surprise, then, to find in an English opera such as Purcell's *Dido and Aeneas* a general Triumphing Dance and an Echo Dance of the Furies in the first act, and a Witches' Dance and several Sailors' Dances in the last. Had native English opera continued to develop in the eighteenth and nineteenth centuries, it might have been as rich in dance as French opera. But a flood of Italian works coupled with a paucity of talented native composers resulted in a withering of English opera so severe that there were few signs of recovery until well into the twentieth century.

Occasional later Italian operas pause long enough for dancers to take the stage. There is a peasants' dance in Giordano's *Andrea Chenier*, and Ponchielli's *Gioconda* contains some of the most notorious ballet music in all opera, the "Dance of the Hours." Verdi's *Aida* has a ritual dance of the Priestesses in the first act, a dance of the young Moorish slaves in the second, and a full-fledged French ballet sequence later in the same act: in a scene of impressive pageantry, the King, priests, officers, standard-bearers, troops, and other miscellaneous persons are collected on stage; so a troupe of dancing girls enters to entertain them, and the audience.

The Russians are fond of ballet, and when indigenous opera finally developed in the later nineteenth century, dance often figured prominently. Tchaikovsky's *Queen of Spades* resorts to the old theatrical trick of a play-within-a-play to introduce dance. The second act takes place in the home of a wealthy aristocrat, with a masked ball underway. Chairs are set before a small stage, and the master of ceremonies summons the guests to watch a pastoral, "The Faithful Shepherdess." Shepherds and shepherdesses appear and do a preliminary dance; they dance a round, to the accompaniment of a chorus; next comes another dance, in contrasting meter; following a duet, this interlude concludes with a finale in which the plot is resolved happily and a minuet and a final round are danced.

Everything stops for a few minutes in the first act of *Der Freischütz* while peasants do a waltz. Even American opera makes occasional use of ballet: the three kings, their retinue, shepherds, and Amahl and his mother sit down and watch in Menotti's *Amahl and the Night Visitors* as a small group of shepherds does a rather extended dance. And some twentieth-century composers have taken advantage of the development of what is loosely called "modern dance," in which the formalized steps and sequences of traditional ballet are replaced by freely invented movements and gestures which can be suited to any dramatic situation. The scene of the Golden Calf near the end of Act II of Schoenberg's *Moses und Aron* contains one of the most spectacular dance sequences in all opera. Horses, camels, and other beasts of burden enter from different sides of the stage, carrying wine, oil, grain, and other materials for a feast. Butchers prepare to slaughter animals, dancing with wild abandon as they sharpen their knives and approach the herds. As night begins to fall, they kill various animals and cut chunks of meat from them, throwing these to the people crowding around. As some gorge themselves on the raw meat, other commence wild dances of destruction and even suicide. Weapons, utensils, and implements are smashed and thrown around the stage as some in the crowd kill themselves with swords, or by leaping from cliffs. Several ignite their clothing and run flaming across the stage. Frenzied dancing of various sorts continues throughout this memorable spectacle.

In general, however, composers of other nationalities have not made as consistent use of dance in opera as have French composers, nor are audiences elsewhere such connoisseurs of dance as the French.

✿ DANCE AS SCENERY

The second act of Tchaikovsky's *Eugene Onegin* takes place in a ballroom. After a waltz, and a song by Triquet, the Captain announces the beginning of the cotillion, the orchestra strikes up a mazurka, and the guests begin to dance. Onegin dances with Olga for a bit, then a quarrel commences between him and Lenski, while the music continues and the other guests dance as a backdrop against which the principal action takes place. Eventually the quarrel leads to a challenge to a duel. Dancing is not used here for its own sake, as a diversion from the main business of the opera, but to contribute to the atmosphere of the scene. It is a part of the scenery, a background for the more important activity in the foreground.

Samuel Barber has a quite similar scene at the beginning of the third act of *Vanessa*. The set depicts the entrance hall of a castle; at the back of the stage is a large archway leading into the ballroom, where a New Year's dance is in progress. Dancing couples can be seen, dance music heard, but this is all in the background. From time to time various of the principals come and go, becoming involved in conversations in the entrance hall. The action is carried forward in these conversations, with the dancing in the ballroom furnishing a constantly shifting backdrop, always subordinate to what is happening in front of it.

The final scene of Verdi's *A Masked Ball* takes place at a masquerade dance, with much of the action, including the climactic murder, played against a backdrop of dancing couples. The third scene of the last act of Berg's *Wozzeck* is set in a tavern, where a wild polka is being danced; some of the dialogue and action take place against this. A country dance celebrating the wedding of Mary and Jabez Stone is in progress when the first curtain goes up in Douglas Moore's *The Devil and Daniel Webster* and continues in the background as some of the main characters are introduced. The first scene of Gounod's *Romeo and Juliet* takes place at a masked ball given by the Capulets.

In each of these scenes, the libretto presents a situation in which people are engaged in social dancing; this is the most important distinction between them and the dance scenes described in the first part of this chapter. Dance as diversion is performed by professionals, who have enough skill, grace, and technique to hold the audience's attention and even arouse their enthusiasm. This is necessary, since nothing else is going on, and all attention is centered on them. But when social dancing is used as a background for more important action, the skill of the dancers is not of such importance. Actually, it should not attract too much attention to itself and away from whatever else is taking place. The dancing in such scenes is often done by members of the chorus, who can usually be taught to perform simple dance steps adequately.

Dance as diversion is performed by a professional *corps de ballets*, dancing as scenery often by members of the chorus. There are also scattered instances of protagonists in the drama being asked to dance. For instance, when Orfeo descends to the underworld in the second act of Gluck's *Orfeo*, a company of Furies bars his way. They first sing to him, inquiring into his reasons for being there, then they are asked to do a dance in which they bar his way. After he has softened their hearts with his impassioned and pathetic singing, they allow him to pass, again dancing as they make way for him. The composer asks that members of the chorus both sing and dance, and in practice this results in the operatic chorus being trained to do a few rudimentary dance steps, rather than dancers being asked to take over the very important choral sections of the scene.

The most spectacular example of a principal singer being asked to dance occurs in Strauss's *Salome*. Herod is fascinated by Salome, his stepdaughter, and begs her to dance for him, telling her that he will give her anything she wishes if she will do it. She finally agrees, with the intention of asking for the head of the imprisoned prophet Jokanaan (John the Baptist), for whom she has conceived a curious and morbid passion. The action and dialogue stop, everyone on stage sits down to watch, and the dance begins. All attention is on Salome's dance, the Dance of the Seven Veils, and there is no way for the singer to "fake" the scene. The dancing must be effective and convincing, or the whole effect of the scene, and possibly of the entire opera, will be spoiled. No matter how well the singer has done her difficult vocal part to this point, her performance will be spoiled if this lengthy solo dance is clumsy or ludicrous. Needless to say, this is a difficult role to cast; the singer must be able to handle an extremely difficult vocal and dramatic part, and also do an effective dance.

In most instances in which principals are asked to dance, the demands are not as great as this; only a few steps of some social dance are required. A scene in the first-act finale of Mozart's *Don Giovanni* is typical. The setting is a ballroom, where a dance has just ended and the guests are returning to their places. After some conversation, three more guests appear, Donna Anna, Donna Elvira, and Don Ottavio; they are looking for Don Giovanni, to revenge the various injuries and indignities they have suffered from him. The latter shouts to the orchestra to play again, a minuet begins, and he dances with the young peasant girl, Zerlina. The various principals sing against this minuet; the Don tries to embrace Zerlina, and finally dances her off stage. Her young boyfriend, Masetto, sees this and starts after them, but Leporello, the Don's servant, seizes him and dances about with him until a scream is heard from outside and the dance stops. Four of the principals must execute the minuet in this sequence, but it does not matter how well they dance. The effect of the scene depends on other things.

The Doctor in Barber's *Vanessa* is called upon to do a few waltz steps, but he is not expected to do these with grace or finesse—to the contrary, he should be awkward and amusing. Baron Ochs in Strauss's *Der Rosenkavalier* does a clumsy parody of a waltz. Some of the principals in *Eugene Onegin* must do a mazurka in one scene and a polonaise in another. Carmen joins the dancing at the conclusion of her "Gypsy Song" which opens the second act of Bizet's opera. But polished dancing is not necessary in any of these sequences. If the singer can do a few steps gracefully, so much the better, but nothing essential is lost if this is not possible, and if a particular singer is unusually clumsy, the staging can be altered a bit to eliminate his dancing altogether.

Talent for singing and dancing is often combined in the same individual, and musical comedy or operetta frequently calls for one or more principals equally talented in the two. There is an excellent reason why major operatic roles seldom call for dancing, however. Rimsky-Korsakov asks the king and the queen to dance in his *Coq d'Or*, but he says in a note at the beginning:

> The dances performed by the King and Queen in the second act must be carried out so as not to interfere with the singers' breathing by too sudden or too violent movement.

Operatic singing is an intensely physical activity. A singer is an athlete who must strengthen certain parts of his body by intensive training and must stay in good physical condition. Singers weakened by illness or insufficient rest may find it impossible to perform satisfactorily; many singers are intensely serious, and even fanatical, about keeping in condition and getting proper rest and nutrition. Dancing is also an intense physical activity. Though ballet dancers, seen from a distance, seem to float through their steps with ease, straining muscles, gasps for breath, and heavy thuds as they hit the floor become apparent upon nearer view. An operatic singer exhausted and out of breath from this sort of activity would have great difficulty

A ballet scene from the fifth act of Meyerbeer's Le Prophete.
This is one of the first photographs taken of an operatic scene.

in singing as well as he could otherwise. Asking a singer to do anything more than a few simple dance steps would endanger his ability to sing to the best of his capabilities. The heart of opera is singing, and it goes against the nature of opera to ask singers to do other things which might affect it adversely.

PANTOMIME AND GESTURE

At the very end of *Der Rosenkavalier* the young lovers, Sophie and Octavian, have been paired off at last and are on stage alone. They embrace, kiss, then run off the stage quickly, hand in hand. The stage is left empty, and the opera is apparently over. But Sophie had dropped her handkerchief during the embrace, and it lies on the middle of the stage. In the words of the libretto:

Then the center door is opened again. Through it comes the little Black Boy, with a taper in his hand;—looks for the handkerchief;—finds it;—picks it up;—trips out.— The curtain falls quickly.

In some ways, this tiny sequence is like a dance; there is no text, and therefore no singing; all attention is centered on the movements of a character on stage, and these movements are accompanied by music and must be synchronized with this music; much of the effectiveness of the scene depends on the attractiveness and appeal with which these movements are executed. It is unlike dance in that the movements and gestures are not based on conventional, stylized steps and positions, but are freely invented for this situation and are more closely related to natural body movements. In ballet and other dance, movements are made to be beautiful in themselves, and a dancer is judged on the grace, ease, and control with which they are executed. But pantomime is used for narrative purposes; it has been described as "prose ballet."

Many operatic composers of the last century or so have conceived their works visually as well as aurally. They have been concerned with what audiences will hear, and also with what they will see. They have realized that stage movement synchronized with music can be a useful and effective tool in narration and in establishing the personalities of their various characters.

The climax of the second act of Puccini's *Tosca* comes when Tosca stabs the villainous Scarpia. But the act does not end here; Tosca is directed to go through the following elaborate pantomime:

Without taking her eyes off Scarpia's corpse she goes to the table, dips a napkin in the water-pitcher and washes her fingers, then arranges her hair before the looking-glass. . . . Remembering the passport, she looks for it on the desk and, not finding it, searches elsewhere; at last she sees it clutched in Scarpia's fingers. . . . She lifts Scarpia's arm, which she lets fall, stiff and inert, when she has taken the passport, which she hides in her bosom. . . . She extinguishes the lights on the table and is about to leave when, seeing one of the candles on the desk still burning, she takes it and lights the other candles with it. . . . She places one candle to the right of Scarpia's head, and the other to the left. . . . She looks around again and, seeing a crucifix hanging on the wall, takes it down and, kneeling, places it on the breast of the corpse. She rises and leaves cautiously, closing the door after her.[1]

These actions are performed against sustained, subdued music. Though specific gestures do not have to be coordinated with certain measures of music, there is only a certain amount of music, and everything must come out together. It has become a tradition for the lighting of the two candles and the placing of the crucifix to be done on three particular chords.

This pantomime is a clever, melodramatic touch, though it is not at all essential to the main thread of the drama. It is a sort of unwinding after the climax of the gory murder of Scarpia; if it were omitted, if Tosca were to rush out immediately after the stabbing, no violence would be done to the dramatic structure of the act.

In other scenes, though, pantomine is used in a narrative way, working with the text or in place of it to move the story line forward. Such a scene must be conceived of in this way from the beginning, of course, with the libretto specifying what stage action is to take place before the composer begins his job. In the concluding scene of Menotti's *The Medium*, for instance, music, text, and pantomime work together to bring the sordid drama to a climax and conclusion. The movements and gestures of the characters, and their positions on the stage, are so essential to a comprehension of what is taking place that the text alone is not sufficient for an understanding of what happens. If the libretto were to be printed with stage directions omitted, or if the opera were to be performed on the radio with no explanation, it would not be at all clear how the drama ends. The situation leading to this final scene is that Madame Flora ("Baba"),

[1] By courtesy of G. Ricordi C., Milan.

an unscrupulous medium, has been frightened by several occurrences in the course of her seances which she cannot explain. Terrified, she searches for some natural cause, accuses her deaf-mute helper Toby of trying to frighten her, whips him, and drives him from the house —to the distress of her daughter Monica, who is in love with Toby. Baba has been drinking, and now she sits at a table, asleep.

> *Toby comes up the stairwell.*
> *Cautiously, he walks tiptoe to Monica's room.*
> *He finds the door locked. He scratches softly on the door.*
> *Baba stirs in her sleep, knocking the bottle down. Toby runs behind the couch, then very slowly creeps out again.*
> *Toby again tries the door. He knocks at it.*
> *The trunk lid falls sharply. Baba wakes up with a start.*
> *Toby hides behind the curtain of the puppet theater.*

BABA: Who's there? Who's there? Answer me!
Monica, Monica, is it you? Who is it then?
If you are human, answer me!
Who is it? Who is it?

> *She takes a revolver out of a drawer in the table.*

BABA: Speak out or I'll shoot! I'll shoot! I'll shoot!
Answer me! Answer me! I'll shoot! I'll shoot!

> *The curtain moves, Baba screams and fires at it several times. For a few seconds everything is completely still. Then very slowly a spot of blood appears on the white curtain and runs down the length of it.*

BABA: I've killed the ghost!

> *Toby's hands are now seen clutching the sides of the curtain. The rod breaks under his weight, and, wrapped, in the curtain, he falls headlong into the room.*

BABA: I've killed the ghost!

> *Monica pounds at the door from within.*

MONICA: Oh! Help! Help! Help!

> *She runs downstairs. The door slams. Baba slowly kneels by Toby.*

BABA: Was it you? Was it you?

> *The curtain falls very slowly.*[2]

Stage directions here take up more space than the text, but there is no break in the music when action is substituting for word: the orchestra accompanies all gestures and movements.

[2] Copyright 1948 by G. Schirmer, Inc.

Most operas from the earlier centuries of the form make little or no use of such stage directions. The drama of the libretto was drama of language, not of movement. Metastasio's libretti often have but one direction in each scene, a simple instruction for one or more of the characters to leave the stage. Occasionally a singer is told to which of the other singers on stage a given line is to be addressed, and there are scattered indications of movement and posture, but mostly the action of the plot and the characterization of the various persons in the drama is clear enough from what is in the text. Monteverdi's *Orfeo* does not have a single stage direction in the entire libretto; whole scenes in Cesti's *Il Pomo d'Oro* go by with none, others have one or two suggesting necessary action; Gluck's operas also go for entire scenes without a direction.

The absence of stage directions in such works does not mean that the visual side of opera was neglected, though. Quite to the contrary. Sets and costumes were often far more lavish than we are accustomed to today, and there was of course movement on the stage, with characters moving on and off, and around the stage while they were on it. And it would have been surprising if the singers had not assumed the roles of the characters they were portraying, and assumed postures and affected gestures and movements appropriate to the emotions spelled out in the text. We know from contemporary criticism that this did happen; some singers were praised as highly for the affecting manner in which they delivered their recitatives and arias as for the actual sound and technique of their voices. In a good libretto of this time, each of the characters in the drama had a distinct personality, suggested in the lines which they delivered in the course of the opera. A good actor-singer would study the libretto and understand what postures and gestures would best suggest a personality, without being told in a series of stage directions. Likewise an understanding of the dramatic situation in each scene, of the relationships of each of the characters to one another, would suggest to the singer how his lines should be delivered; he will not need such instructions as "angrily," or "with increasing intensity," or "casually, yet with a suggestion of suspicion." And the text of a libretto of this period also makes it clear what movement is necessary. If a character who has not been involved in the drama has a line to deliver, he must make an entrance sometime before the time for this line; if someone says "Look! Marcellus and Philidor fight!" there is no need of a stage direction saying "Marcellus and Philidor fight." If Marcellus says "Hold! I am dying!" it is clear enough what must happen during the fight.

As might be expected, there is a parallel situation in spoken drama. Stage directions in Shakespearean plays are infrequent and brief. Stage movement, postures, gestures, and manner of delivery must be deduced from a careful reading of the text. Climaxes take place in language, not in physical action. A consequence of this fact is that actors and directors have a considerable amount of latitude in their interpretation of details of action and characterization, and different productions of the same play may vary widely in external details. By contrast, more recent plays tend to have extensive stage directions, descriptions of sets and lighting effects, and detailed instructions for the actors' movements, gestures, and even facial expressions. Climaxes may take place in scenes of physical action, with the actors either silent or uttering unpoetic exclamations. In some extreme instances, drama through language is almost supplanted by the idea of drama through movement, and theater moves close to some sort of modern dance with incidental words.

Prescription of action and gestures in opera librettos has also become more common in the last century and a half. New librettos have been more liberally sprinkled with such instructions, and new editions of older operas have been brought in line with the spirit of the times by the addition of stage directions not found in the original. In the following scene from the first act of Mozart's *Don Giovanni*, the stage directions to the left are those found in Mozart's own score, those to the right are taken from an edition prepared in the early part of the present century.

Sees the corpse.   *Seeing the corpse.*

DONNA ANNA: What is this I behold? Can I believe my senses?
Ah unhappy me!

Sinks down beside the body.

My father, oh my father, look but upon me!

Throws herself upon the corpse.

DON OTTAVIO: My lord!

DONNA ANNA: Ah, by that villain he has been slain.

Examining the corpse more carefully.

He's bleeding—from this wound here—
His face too wears now the livid pallor of the dying!

Don Ottavio offers to raise her; she refuses.

I cannot feel him breathe; how cold his hands are!

She rises.

Father dear, father dear, father, oh father!

She reels.

Oh help me—

Don Ottavio supports her, and leads her to the stone seat.

I'm fainting!

Faints, swoons.   *She faints.*

DON OTTAVIO: *To the servants.*

Go fetch a surgeon quickly, we may still save him.
You women there, bring cordials, lay her down, gently!

A maid servant hurries into the palace, and returns immediately with a smelling bottle, which she offers to Donna Anna.

Is no one coming? Donna Anna! Dearest! Oh hear me!
Has such great sorrow broken her heart forever?

DONNA ANNA:
Revives, arises
Ah!

DON OTTAVIO: She recovers; what can be done to help her?

DONNA ANNA: *With a deep sigh.*
Where is my father?

DON OTTAVIO: *To servants.*

Go quickly, bear away the body of your master;
It will distress her to see it.

The Commandant is carried away.   *Serving-men raise the Commandant, and bear him to the palace.*

Oh my beloved! Be comforted, take courage.

DONNA ANNA: *Despairingly.*   *Springing up and repulsing Don Ottavio as if insane.*

Leave me, I pray you, leave me.
Here let me end my sorrows.

Singers of the late eighteenth or early nineteenth century would have supplied many of the actions specified in the later score in the course of "interpreting" the role; but not being bound by one set of such precise instructions, they might have made somewhat different movements and gestures which they considered more effective. The point here is that stage action in this scene does not add anything to the dramatic situation, which is quite clearly laid out in the text. The flow of the action can be followed from a reading of the words alone; physical action on the stage merely pictures it.

We see a quite different situation in a scene such as the following one which opens the first act of Wagner's *Die Walküre*. Though the skeleton of the action can be followed in the text, the liberally supplied stage directions give details of characterization and subtleties of plot development which the librettist-composer considered necessary for an accurate realization of his drama.

> *Siegmund opens the entrance door from without and enters. He holds the latch in his hand and looks around the room; he appears exhausted with over-exertion; his dress and appearance show that he is in flight. Seeing no one, he closes the door behind him, walks, as with the last efforts of an exhausted man, to the hearth, and there throws himself down on a rug of bearskin.*

SIEGMUND: Whoe'er owns this hearth, here must I rest me.

> *He sinks back and remains stretched out motionless. Sieglinde enters from the inner chamber, thinking that her husband has returned. Her grave looks show surprise when she finds a stranger stretched out on the hearth.*

SIEGLINDE: *Still at back.*

A stranger here? I must question him.

> *She comes nearer.*

Who is this who came in the house,
And lies there on the hearth?

> *As Siegmund does not move, she comes still nearer and looks at him.*

Worn and way-weary lies he there.
Is it but weariness, or is he sick?

> *She bends over and listens.*

He is still breathing, yet his eyes are closed.
The man seems valiant; he fell only from exhaustion.

SIEGMUND: *Suddenly raising his head.*

A drink! A drink!

SIEGLINDE: I will bring you refreshment.

> *She quickly takes a drinking horn and goes out. She returns with it filled and offers it to Siegmund.*

SIEGLINDE: Drink to moisten thy lips I have brought thee;
Water, as thou didst wish!

> *Siegmund drinks and gives the horn back. As he acknowledges his thanks with his head, his eyes fix themselves on her with growing interest.*[3]

---

[3] Translation by Frederick Jameson.

Here the composer has created not only music, but also the exact visual spectacle which this music accompanies. It is only a short step from a scene such as this to one in which stage action furnishes dramatic material not even hinted at in the text, as in the scene from Menotti's *The Medium* discussed earlier.

⚜ SUMMARY

Most of the earlier operas had dance sequences, but it was the French who were most enthusiastic about dance and retained it as an essential feature of their operas. At first, dance was treated as pure diversion, with dramatic action stopping for a sequence of dances; later, composers often tried to integrate dance scenes into the flow of action. Dance remained an integral part of French opera into the present century, and English and Russian operas also have made frequent use of it. It was used more sporadically in Italian and German opera, but whenever works by composers of these nationalities were given in France, dance sequences were introduced to make them more palatable to the French taste.

Dancing is most often done by professional dancers, but on occasion the chorus and even certain of the principals are asked to execute simple dances, usually social dances, as part of the stage picture.

The drama in opera was originally developed in the text of the libretto, with stage directions used sparingly. Movement on the stage, and gestures and pantomime, were developed by individual performers and directors to picture and intensify dramatic details, from a reading of the libretto. But more recently, composers themselves have been more concerned with the stage picture, and have specified the precise movements which they want to accompany lines of text, and in some instances even resorted to narrative pantomime to supply elements of the drama not made explicit in the text.

OPERA AND MUSIC DRAMA

The various component parts of an opera have been discussed one by one to this point, and the next chapter will analyze an entire act of one opera to demonstrate how these are combined and contrasted in a complete work. The present chapter is an intermediate one, raising some general questions of structure and the integration of the smaller units of an opera into a satisfactory large form.

Opera, almost from its inception, has fluctuated between two rather different concepts, two polarities, which are often referred to as *opera* (or *number opera*) and *music drama*. Most operas fall, stylistically, somewhere between these two poles, drawing some ideas from one and some from the other; but for purposes of illustration let us examine briefly a work which represents a rather extreme instance of one concept, then one which just as clearly illustrates the other.

Domenico Cimarosa's *Il Matrimonio Segreto*, to a libretto by Giovanni Bertati, was first performed in Vienna in 1792. Though it is called a *"Melodramma giocoso,"* it is an excellent and charming example of a work constructed according to the conventions of "opera," as opposed to those of "music drama."

The first act is preceded by a *Sinfonia*, in D major. After a tiny *largo* beginning of three sets of loud chords, the *allegro moderato* section which comprises the body of the overture commences. Formally, the overture is a somewhat loosely constructed piece in sonata-allegro form. The two major themes are clear enough, and are stated in the usual keys, but the exposition is episodic, with new thematic material and modulations appearing unexpectedly, and the development section is brief and less eventful than one would expect to find in a purely symphonic work of this sort. Nevertheless, the overture is a complete composition, self-contained musically and coming to a resounding and convincing close.

The first act opens with an Introduction involving Carolina and Paolino, who are secretly married. This is a dramatically static duet, with the two expressing affection for one another; after an orchestral prelude, Paolino sings the principal theme, Carolina answers him with the same music, the two sing in more rapid alternation and finally together, and the scene ends with a change to a slightly faster tempo for a brief codetta in which the two sing mostly in parallel thirds. There is a full cadence in the key in which the duet began, B♭ major.

A section of *secco* recitative between the two furnishes some necessary information: Geronimo, Carolina's father, does not know of the marriage of the two, and being financially ambitious, wishes to make "good" matches for Carolina and her older sister Elisetta. Carolina leaves, but not before the two have sung a short duet in C major, again with an instrumental introduction leading into a statement of the main melodic material by Carolina, a repetition of it by Paolino, and a closing section in which they sing together.

More characters enter in the following recitative scene (Geronimo, Elisetta, and Geronimo's sister Fidalma). Geronimo asks everyone to listen to an important announcement, in a short section of accompanied recitative, then sings an aria in which he tells them that he has arranged a marriage for Elisetta, to no less a personage than a real count.

The three women are left on the stage with Geronimo's exit, and the two sisters begin bickering, with Fidalma attempting to arbitrate and calm them. After this situation is clearly drawn in recitative, the three commence a trio. The structure is bisectional: first the three sing consecutively, with Carolina stating the melody first, Elisetta echoing her, and Fidalma attempting to quiet them when her turn comes; the second section is faster, with the three answering one another in quick, sometimes overlapping passages, and finally singing together for the climax.

Carolina leaves, and the other two converse in recitative, in which we learn that Fidalma is infatuated with Paolino. She sings an aria in which she speaks of the joys of having a husband; as before, an instrumental prelude leads into the aria, which changes to a faster tempo at midpoint for a spirited and florid conclusion.

Now Count Robinson, Elisetta's intended husband, enters and is introduced in a recitative scene. He sings a pompous and windy aria in praise of the two girls; the other five principals function as a chorus, expressing wonderment at his behavior when he pauses for breath. Again, a brief orchestral coda brings this section to a full cadence before the next section begins.

The plot takes a critical turn in the next section of recitative: the Count has been charmed with Carolina, and assumed that she is his bride-to-be, but now Fidalma informs him that it is Elisetta whom he is to marry. His consternation is apparent, and an ensemble-quartet follows, in which the Count, Elisetta, Carolina, and Fidalma in turn ruminate on this turn of events. They sing consecutively at first, then in various combinations, and the first section of the quartet works to a climax in which all four sing their different texts together. The tempo changes from *largo* to *allegro moderato* for the second half of the ensemble, in which the four sing first by pairs and then quickly work to the point of singing together to bring this section to a rousing conclusion.

Paolino and Carolina are alone in the next scene; a few exchanges in recitative lead to a brilliant, florid aria by Paolino. This one is short, in one tempo (*allegro con brio*) throughout, and is preceded by a section of accompanied recitative.

Carolina leaves, the Count enters, and the next twist of the plot develops in recitative when the latter tells Paolino that he has decided to marry the younger daughter (Carolina), and will accept a lesser dowry if the father will agree to this change of plans. A duet follows, and since the two are in different emotional states, they do not share the same melodic material—as they have in the earlier ensemble scenes—but are given vocal lines appropriate to their moods. Paolino sings a legato, expressive line which matches his unhappy, apprehensive state, while the Count, delighted at the prospect of having a younger, more attractive bride than he had expected, is given an active, leaping, rapidly declaimed line. As in earlier ensembles, the two sing consecutively, then together, and there is a change to a more rapid tempo near the end of the section.

The next scene involves the Count and Carolina. He tells her of his plan to marry her rather than her sister, and in the ensuing aria she attempts to dissuade him by enumerating her various deficiencies: she claims she has a poor figure, is frivolous, ill at ease, lacks social graces, and speaks neither French, Spanish, nor German.

The act ends with a finale, an extended one made up of a

series of shorter ensembles strung together. After a bit of preliminary recitative, Geronimo, Elisetta, Fidalma, and Paolino sing an ensemble-quartet, built in the usual way with the four singing one by one at first, then in various pairs, and finally all four together at the end. Now Carolina and the Count enter; he has been trying to persuade her to marry him, and Elisetta and Fidalma enter into the discussion to make it a quartet. Next follows a scene in which all six principals sing, mostly in dialogue fashion, one after another, and the final section of the finale is a sextet in which all six sing together most of the time, bringing the act to a spirited conclusion.

Each of the scenes in this act, then, is a separate unit in itself, beginning and ending in the same key, having some satisfactory form, and clearly marked off by strong cadences. Any one of these scenes could be taken out of the opera and performed as a concert number, without any changes whatsoever. An opera of this sort is conceived as a succession of separate numbers, each of which makes perfect musical sense itself. Unity is supplied by the plot, and in this case by key relationships among the various sections. Each "number" has its own thematic material, which is not carried over to any other section, and each maintains a characteristic type of text setting: the recitative sections contain nothing but recitative, the aria sections never lapse into recitative, spoken dialogue, or melo-drama, but are in song or a more florid aria style throughout. Variety is achieved by the use of different keys, meters, and tempi for different sections, and by alternation of arias with duets, trios, and quartets, but within any one section there is unity—unity of key, melodic material, form, type of setting, tempo, and meter. The twelve "numbers" of the act are:

1.	Sinfonia (Overture)	D
2.	Introduction: Carolina, Paolino ("Cara, non dubitar")	B♭
3.	Recitative—Duet: Carolina, Paolino ("Io ti lascio")	C
4.	Recitative—Aria: Geronimo ("Udite, tutti udite")	D
5.	Recitative—Trio: Carolina, Elisetta, Fidalma ("Le faccio un inchino")	G
6.	Recitative—Aria: Fidalma ("È vero che in casa")	F
7.	Recitative—Aria with Chorus: Count ("Senza tante cerimonie")	F

Richard Strauss's *Salome* is a setting of the play by Oscar Wilde; it was first performed in Dresden in 1905. It is evident from even a cursory examination of either the score or the libretto that the organization of this work is radically different from that of the Cimarosa opera just discussed. The obvious differences in the libretto are that the various characters converse with no clear differentiation between information-giving passages and those of a more reflective, lyric nature and that no single character has more than a few sentences before another speaks. This structure is reflected in the music by the absence of extended sections for individual singers (though there are a few exceptions which will be noted) and the complete absence of sections in which two or more of the characters sing simultaneously. Some of the unique characteristics of opera have been given up for structures which are similar to those of spoken drama.

The setting is a terrace in the palace of King Herod. We see, when the curtain rises after only a few bars of music, a young Syrian (Narraboth), a page, several soldiers, and a Cappadocian. A banquet is in progress inside, and the characters on stage comment on the sights and sounds from the hall, in conversational style. Narraboth is interested only in Salome, the stepdaughter of Herod, and it is apparent from his first lines that he is infatuated with her. He speaks only of her, and what he has to say could be the text for an aria in an "opera."

NARRABOTH: How beautiful is the Princess Salome to-night!

.   .   .   .   .

    She has a strange look. She is like a princess who has little white doves for feet. One might fancy she was dancing.

How beautiful is the Princess Salome to-night!

She is very beautiful to-night.

How pale the Princess is! Never have I seen her so pale.
She is like the shadow of a white rose in a mirror of silver.

The Princess is getting up! She is leaving the table! She
looks very troubled. Ah, she is coming this way.

Yes, she is coming towards us.

She is like a dove that has strayed.

Laid out in this way, Narraboth's words appear to be suitable
for an aria text. But his phrases are sometimes separated by several
pages of other music: the Page speaks of the strange appearance of
the moon, and of a premonition that something terrible will happen;
the soldiers comment on the Jews inside who are quarreling about
religion; the voice of Jokanaan is heard rising from the cistern in
which he is imprisoned; and the soldiers and the Cappadocian comment on Jokanaan. At times the various singers have contrasting
musical material, appropriate to their texts, but since each sings so
briefly, there is no time for development of these ideas. At other
times the music flows along in its own way, with the same sort of
melodic and harmonic material being used for different singers and
contrasting lines of text. There is often a contrast between recitative-
like setting, with information-bearing lines of text declaimed in a
syllabic, melodically inexpressive style, and arioso-like setting, with
more highly charged text sung to expressive music, often with some
trace of melodic development as in the example shown opposite.[1]

The general impression one has of this section of the opera
is of freely unfolding music not chopped up into sections, of different bits of melodies and various types of text settings alternating
so rapidly, with little articulation, that the forward thrust of the
music and drama carries the audience along without pause.

Now Salome comes onto the terrace, and for the first time one
character is given a somewhat extended section of continuous text,
without interruption. Superficially, this appears to be an aria, and
this suggests that what has come before is in the nature of an

extended recitative section. But neither the text nor the music behave as they should in an aria in a traditional "opera."

SALOME: I will not stay. I cannot stay. Why does the Tetrarch look at me all the while with his mole's eyes under his shaking eyelids? It is strange that the husband of my mother looks at me like that.

How sweet is the air here! I can breathe here! Within there are Jews from Jerusalem who are tearing each other in pieces over their foolish ceremonies, and Egyptians silent and subtle, and Romans brutal and coarse, with their uncouth jargon. Ah! how I loathe the Romans!

.   .   .   .   .

How good to see the moon! She is like a little silver flower, cold and chaste. I am sure she is a virgin. She has never defiled herself.

This is not reflection on action which has preceded it; it is not a static moment in the drama; nor does the text fall into some symmetrical poetical form, as usually happens in an aria. The music is not constructed of balanced phrases falling into some recognizable pattern; a series of melodic ideas is presented, with no repetition, and in changing of meters and tempi. If this section were lifted out of the opera and sung by itself, it would make no particular musical sense. It makes sense, musically and dramatically, only in context, as one episode in a continuously unfolding stream of words and music. Wilde's drama unfolds in prose: lines of text are not matched in meter or length, nor is there any scheme of rhyme. Strauss, taking this technique as a guide, wrote music which also unfolds freely and flexibly, following the dictates of the text; he does not impose formal musical structures on sections of text which do not fall into symmetrical, recurrent patterns themselves.

A bit later, however, there is an extended passage in the play which is not unlike an operatic scene in structure. A relatively static moment has been reached: Salome has heard the voice of Jokanaan coming from the well, has asked that he be brought up to the terrace, tries to converse with him, and finds herself becoming morbidly fascinated with him. The text at this point reads very much like that of an operatic duet: two characters have been brought, in the text leading up to this point, to rather obvious and static dramatic states, and they express themselves for awhile in language which is designed to be of interest in itself, not to carry the drama further.

SALOME: Jokanaan! I am amorous of thy body, Jokanaan! Thy body is white like the lilies of a field that the mower hath never mowed. Thy body is white like the snows that lie on the mountains of Judea. The roses in the garden of the Queen of Arabia are not so white as thy body. Neither the roses of the garden of the Queen of Arabia, nor the feet of the dawn when they light on the leaves, nor the breath of the moon when she lies on the breast of the sea. . . . There is nothing in the world so white as thy body. Suffer me to touch thy body.

JOKANAAN: Back! daughter of Babylon! By woman came evil into the world. Speak not to me. I will not listen to thee. I listen but to the voice of the Lord God.

SALOME: Thy body is hideous. It is like the body of a leper. It is like a plastered wall where vipers have crawled; like a plastered wall where the scorpions have made their nest. It is like a whitened sepulchre full of loathsome things. It is horrible, thy body is horrible. It is thy hair that I am enamoured of, Jokanaan. Thy hair is like clusters of grapes, like the clusters of black grapes that hang from the vine-trees of Edom in the land of the Edomites. . . . There is nothing in the world that is so black as thy hair. Suffer me to touch thy hair.

JOKANAAN: Back, daughter of Sodom! Touch me not. Profane not the temple of the Lord God.

SALOME: Thy hair is horrible. It is covered with mire and dust. It is like a knot of serpents coiled round thy neck. I love not thy hair. It is thy mouth that I desire, Jokanaan. Thy mouth is like a band of scarlet on a tower of ivory. It is like a pomegranate cut in twain with a knife of ivory. . . . There is nothing in the world so red as thy mouth. Suffer me to kiss thy mouth.

JOKANAAN: Never! daughter of Babylon! Daughter of Sodom! Never.

SALOME: I will kiss thy mouth, Jokanaan. I will kiss thy mouth.

The music to which Strauss has set this scene is no more and no less tightly organized than the text. Where Wilde has repeated lines, or has lines which are clearly parallel, Strauss has written music with recognizable motifs, rhythmic or melodic, or both.[2]

[2] Copyright 1905 by Adolph Furstner; renewed 1933. Renewal Copyright assigned to Boosey & Hawkes, Inc., 1943. Reprinted by permission.

Sehr lebhaft   SALOME

In dein Haar_____ bin ich ver-liebt,_____   Jo -

cha - na - an.

But these melodic and rhythmic similarities are shortwinded, and the subsequent lines of text continue to unfold freely, each in its own way, without turning back to repeat or vary the melodic material with which they began and without making melodic reference to other sections of the scene. The music of this lengthy scene has the same forward thrust mentioned earlier, the same momentum, the same drive from one section to another with no hint of repose or of turning back to repeat or vary or round off something which has happened earlier in the music. We see the same restlessness when we attempt an analysis of the key scheme of this—or any other— scene. To begin with, there is so much tonal ambiguity, so much modulation, that it is frequently difficult to assign a given passage to any one key. The impression, rather, is of constant movement around and through a number of keys. Some guide is furnished by the key signatures, though, and in the scene between Salome and Jokanaan just discussed the first large section (beginning with "Jokanaan! I am amorous of thy body . . .") has a key signature of B major; the second (beginning with "Thy body is hideous . . .") moves to C major, then to D♭ major; the section beginning "Thy hair is horrible" is so ambiguous and unstable that the composer has assigned it no key signature; and with "It is thy mouth . . ."

we come to a signature suggesting E major. There is no semblance here of the sort of plan whereby a central key is stated and established, keys related to it are introduced, and eventually the original key returns. There is, rather, a sort of stepwise climbing through unrelated keys, which contributes to the general feeling of forward progression and intensification without turning back which is so characteristic of this opera. We see this same device a bit later when Salome reiterates her phrase "Suffer me to kiss thy mouth" several times, each time a step higher.[3]

There are two points, later in the opera, at which Strauss has written prolonged sections of music which can be extracted from the opera. The first of these is Salome's Dance of the Seven Veils; the play simply directs that Salome dance at this point, and the composer has written an instrumental piece which develops musically just as any of his other instrumental music would, since there is no text here to impose its structure and content on the music. The other is Salome's final scene, in which she sings to the severed head of Jokanaan. Here the dramatist has written an extended monologue for a single character, elaborating a single dramatic situation, and the composer has responded by setting this to music which has a clear beginning, which makes some use of thematic repetition, which

[3] Copyright 1905 by Adolph Furstner; renewed 1933. Renewal Copyright assigned to Boosey & Hawkes, Inc., 1943. Reprinted by permission.

moves to a climax, and which comes to an effective close with the singer at the very bottom of her range against somber, slow-moving chords. This is the only instance in the entire opera of an extended section for one of the singers which has a clear beginning and end, and which makes a great deal of musical sense between. It is almost some sort of aria, and has been sung effectively as a concert piece—but Strauss wrote it only because the drama which he was using as a libretto demanded such a piece.

With these exceptions, the music unfolds steadily without clear articulation into "numbers." Certain melodic and rhythmic motives recur from time to time, but not for the purpose of organizing a given section of the music into some traditional musical pattern; they are more associative in nature, and may appear in a voice or in the accompaniment. Strauss draws on almost all of the techniques of text setting, from declaimed recitative-like writing to aria style, but these are not sectionalized and there is often a rapid shift from one to another in the course of a single section or even a single line of text.

Summarizing the distinctions between these two vastly different works: the first is constructed of a chain of numbers, each tonally, melodically, and formally complete, while the second progresses through a series of fluid, flexible, variable, smaller sections which lead directly from one to another and rarely make any sort of musical sense themselves. Segregation is the most important principle of the first, with the effectiveness of the whole opera dependent upon the strength of a succession of almost independent smaller parts, while the notion of integration rules the second, with all component parts—music and text, singing and orchestral playing, poetry and gesture, sets and dance—subjugated to the total effect. These are the external differences, manifestations of a profound difference at the very root of the two works: one is built according to principles of structure which had developed within the form of opera, and are peculiar to it, while the other takes as its guide the conventions and traditions of spoken drama.

The very first operas, those by members of the Florentine Camerata and by Monteverdi and his contemporaries, are often referred to as music dramas. They were of course based on the forms and conventions of contemporary drama and poetry; opera was too new a form to have established its own traditions. But as the seventeenth century wore on and more composers and librettists wrote operas, certain styles, structures, and procedures were developed and standardized, some of them quite different from those of traditional

Salome and Jochanaan, in Strauss's Salome. A Metropolitan Opera Production of 1964–65, with Birgit Nilsson as Salome and William Dooley as Jochanaan.

drama. The eighteenth century saw the peak of the development of the "number opera"; both serious and comic works were constructed according to rather rigid formal procedures, though there were some signs of growing dissatisfaction in the last few decades of the century. The nineteenth century saw a progression from traditional attitudes toward operatic structure in the early years, through various attempts to loosen up traditional forms, to more extreme experimentation by Wagner and others, and finally in the last decades (and carrying over into the present century) to such works as *Salome* and Debussy's *Pelléas et Mélisande* which are quite remote from the number opera of the eighteenth century. The twentieth century has been one of confusion, with some composers attempting to carry the concept of music drama even further, others consciously reverting to the older structures (Stravinsky's *The Rake's Progress* is a striking example of this), and still others attempting some synthesis of the two concepts.

Thus the movement back and forth between the polarities of number opera and music drama can be seen as a chronological phenomenon. But there is more to the history of the form than this. There has been modification on the basis of nationality: in almost all periods, French opera has been inclined toward music drama, probably because French librettists have had closer ties with spoken drama than have their contemporaries in other countries; while Italian opera has clung tenaciously to at least a semblance of traditional "number" structure even in those periods when composers elsewhere were moving completely away from it. Needless to say, there has also been modification of the general chronological development by individual composers. Mozart's mature works are more inclined to music drama than are operas by his lesser contemporaries; Strauss's *Der Rosenkavalier* points the way back to certain traditions of "opera" at the very time when other composers were imitating his *Salome*; Handel's later operas held fast to the traditions of the classical eighteenth-century number opera, though some of his contemporaries were testing ways of breaking away from these.

Finally, it must be emphasized again that even though "number opera" and "music drama" have been presented here as two almost contradictory approaches to the problem of constructing a large musical-dramatic work, most operas, particularly of the past several centuries, represent some sort of compromise between the two. Works which are obviously number operas, with the various sections listed and numbered on the first page of the score, usually make use of some of the more flexible techniques of music drama within certain of these numbers, or between them; and even those works called music dramas by their composers and written with a continuous flow of music which does not pause for the beginnings and endings of arias and ensembles often, upon closer examination, prove to have drawn more on the traditional techniques of opera than the composer himself would care to admit.

Verdi's *La Traviata*, for instance, is a number opera in Italian tradition, and the division into numbers is marked in the score by the composer himself. Yet it is quite different from the Cimarosa work discussed above. The first, most obvious, difference is that each act is made up of fewer numbers, and that each of these is longer and more complex than those of earlier operas. The second act is divided into five numbers, the third into four, and the first only two, an Introduction and a concluding Scene and Aria.

The first section of the first act, the Introduction, will serve as an illustration of how this work is constructed. It can be broken down into four sections itself: an opening, in A major; a brindisi (drinking song) in B♭ major; a waltz, in E♭ major; and a final *stretta* in A♭. But there is much more flexibility than this outline would suggest. The first section begins with a brief section for chorus; after only a few measures, Violetta sings several phrases in arioso style, answered by Flora and the Marquis; a few more measures for chorus and some of the principals leads to the entrance of two more characters, Gastone and Alfredo; Gastone sings two phrases and is answered by a phrase from Violetta; the Marquis, Alfredo, Gastone, and Violetta exchange a few remarks, in expressive recitative style; the chorus has 4 measures, then 4 more measures after the orchestra has accompanied some stage business; Gastone and Violetta engage in a brief conversation, which soon involves several other singers; the chorus and the massed principals exchange exhortations to drink more; Gastone, Alfredo, and Violetta converse for a few phrases; then there is a general shout, requesting Alfredo to sing a drinking song. The techniques here are remarkably like those of music drama: there is rapid exchange between characters, with no single melodic idea developed; chordal writing for the chorus and various types of recitative and arioso alternate freely, often measure by measure. The dramatic function of this section is to introduce the main characters and have them engage in conversation which will begin to establish their personalities and relationships to one another. Though it begins and ends in the same key, and is marked off by strong cadences and double bars in the music, it makes little musical sense isolated from the entire scene.

The drinking song which follows is developed more along musical lines, with a simple melody stated, repeated, given to Violetta, and finally sung by Alfredo and Violetta, accompanied by the chorus and other principals. But again, though the tune is attractive and this section is clearly marked off from what precedes and follows it, it is too brief and there is too little development of the single melodic idea for this part of the opera to be able to lead an independent musical life divorced from the opera.

The waltz section begins with the chorus singing as a background to the conversation of Violetta and several of the other characters. But soon everyone but Violetta and Alfredo leaves, and the music of the waltz continues with the two singing a duet against it. There is a contrasting middle section, extremely florid and in another key and meter, and the duet concludes with a return to the original key and melody. Alfredo leaves, everyone else returns, and the Introduction concludes with a spirited *stretta* in which the chorus and five of the principals sing together, mostly in block chords.

Despite the division into four clearly defined sections, the effect of this Introduction (which takes up two-thirds of the entire act) is of a continual forward movement of music and drama, of a succession of episodes which are themselves constructed in a somewhat episodic fashion, of the juxtaposition of various techniques of text setting within a single section, and of a continuous unfolding of musical ideas appropriate to the various dramatic situations.

Wagner's *Die Walküre*, on the other hand, is commonly regarded as a "music drama"; Wagner thought of his librettos as dramas suitable for presentation without musical setting, and there is little apparent evidence of traditional operatic structures such as arias, ensembles, and the like. But again, closer examination indicates more dependence on these forms than is generally suggested in discussions of this opera.

The first act is made up of three scenes: Siegmund and Sieglinde are alone in the first and third, Hunding joins them in the second. There are the expected obvious differences from an "opera": the score gives no hint of division into "numbers"; the vocal line flows freely from recitative to arioso, and back; the performers sing one at a time, never two or three together; there is no chorus and no dance, but the score is heavily marked with stage directions for pantomime and gesture to accompany words or to substitute for them.

The first scene is almost completely expository, introducing the two main characters in the drama and offering necessary information about them. They converse, mostly in stylized recitative patterns, with the orchestra furnishing most of the melodic interest—and also much information, through the use of leitmotifs. The second scene begins with the entrance of Hunding; much of this scene also progresses in recitative-like vocal phrases, against an expressive orchestra, but Siegmund has one extended section in which he explains the series of events which brought him to the hut. Some of this narration is done in a more expressive recitative style, occasionally bordering on arioso, but there is no suggestion of any symmetrical musical form. Simple recitative patterns dominate the beginning of the third scene, but with the reentrance of Sieglinde the character of the music begins to change: the leitmotif figures are taken more and more by the voices, the range increases, and the two singers are given more extended phrases in place of the short, fragmentary lines they have been singing to this point. This change in the music reflects a change which is taking place in the libretto, in which more lyric, expansive poetry replaces the short, conversational phrases that have made up the bulk of the text to this point.

The door leading outside swings open, brilliant moonlight floods the room, the music modulates suddenly and dramatically to B♭, and with Siegmund's line *"Winterstürme wichen dem Wonnemond"* there begins an extended section which can only be classified as a duet. The character of the music is quite different from what has come before, with balanced, symmetrical phrases and even some repetition of melodic material. Siegmund's first phrases, for example, fall into a quite simple ABBAA form, each phrase being 4 measures, and there is much exchange of melodic material between the two as the duet progresses. (See the example on page 214.)

The music moves through a succession of keys, sometimes reverting briefly to a more declamatory style but soon moving back to the lyric-dramatic arioso style which characterizes this section. Finally Siegmund pulls the sword from the ash tree in which it had been imbedded, the music soars to a climax, and the act ends.

This duet is perhaps too dependent on the form of the text, and makes too much use of the technique of a string of musical ideas prompted by this text, to be perfectly satisfactory as a piece of music, divorced from the rest of the act. But the act progresses from narrative, set in a flexible recitative style, to more reflective text, set in arioso and aria style, and it is possible to regard the entire act as a large recitative-duet structure, enormously expanded but still recognizable. And this not surprising. Wagner acquired a thorough and practical knowledge of "traditional" opera, and patterned his first works after the operas of the men he most admired.

Allmälich bewegter
SIEGMUND

O süs - ses-te Won - ne!

se - lig-stes Weib!

SIEGLINDE

O lass in Nä - he

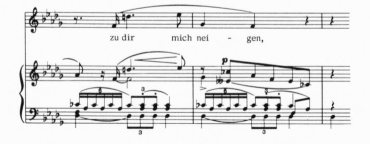

zu dir mich nei - gen,

His prose writings are full of praise of Beethoven, Gluck, Mozart, and even Meyerbeer. *Rienzi*, for instance, is squarely in the tradition of nineteenth-century opera. When he had acquired enough skill in the handling of the materials of opera he began writing works of more striking individuality, and his essays on drama and opera expound some apparently radical notions about musical-dramatic works. But like all great composers, his art was based firmly on the practice of those who had preceded him, and in the perspective of history we can see, more clearly than did his contemporaries, that he expanded and enriched this practice, but never broke with it.

Mussorgsky's *Boris Godunov* will serve as a final example. Often referred to as a music drama, it is constructed of a series of *tableaux*, each with a different stage setting and each built in a flexible dramatic structure, with characters coming and going and various types of music alternating. Perhaps the most dramatic *tableau* is the one near the end of the opera, culminating with the death of Boris; its structure is typical of the composer's method in this work. Even though the music is more or less continuous, and it is not customary to break the *tableaux* into sections in discussions of this opera, this one falls clearly into six major divisions, of varying lengths.

1. A 17-measure orchestral prelude opens the *tableau*. The curtain goes up on a great room in the Kremlin, with a council of boyars meeting in a special session; the prelude sets a solemn mood, which will prevail throughout much of the *tableau*, with a hint near the end of the bells which will ring at the close of the scene.

2. The boyars discuss what punishment should be meted out to the pretender who is agitating against the rule of Boris. Individuals speak, one by one, then all sing together at the end of this brief section.

3. Shuisky enters. After a few lines of conversation, set in simple recitative style, Shuisky tells, in a dramatic narrative, how he has just seen Boris suffering from an apparent hallucination, trembling, perspiring, and calling out to phantoms.

4. Boris enters and converses with Shuisky, who tells him that someone has asked to see him. The aged monk Pimen enters, and tells a tale of how he was visited by an old herdsman, who recounted a miracle: blind, his sight had been restored by a visit to the tomb of Dmitri, the former child Tsar whom Boris had murdered in order to seize power. Boris falls, in a faint.

5. Boris is revived, asks that his son Feodor be brought to him, and dismisses the boyars. He tells Feodor that he is dying, and gives him advice on how to conduct himself as Tsar.

6. Bells sound outside, an offstage chorus chants a funeral dirge, and Boris gasps out a few last words before he falls back dead on his throne.

Each of these smaller sections is marked off by double bars and clear cadences, each has its own melodic material which is not carried over to the following sections, most of them end in the key in which they began, and most begin with simple recitative-like writing and work to a more melodic and expressive recitative and arioso setting, with some repetition of material and suggestions of symmetrical musical structures. Thus the *tableau* is built of a succession of parts, each making some sense taken by itself; obviously it owes much to the history and traditions of "opera." Yet none of these parts is long enough, nor developed enough musically, to be considered a separate "number" (though several of them are sometimes strung together, with the parts of the chorus and other principals eliminated, and performed by a bass soloist as "The Death of Boris"). Each makes much more sense in the context of the entire *tableau*, and it is a telling commentary on the composer's attitude toward the composition of a musical-dramatic work that the *tableau* ends with a minimum of musical interest, but with a climax of dramatic intensity. In this work, the techniques of opera and music drama are so blended that it makes little sense to classify it as one or the other.

CONCLUSION

The concepts of "number opera" (a work constructed of a series of self-contained musical numbers) and "music drama" (one in which the conventions of opera are given up in favor of a continuously unfolding musical-dramatic work, without divisions into separate numbers) are useful ones, enabling us to discuss the structure of opera in a way which probes its essential nature. Certain works fit neatly and convincingly into one category or the other. But many operas, certainly most of those in the current standard repertoire, draw on both techniques, and it is often misleading to attempt to classify them flatly as one type or the other.

SUMMATION:
OPERA AS MUSIC AND DRAMA

Earlier chapters have discussed methods of text setting, the fundamental recitative-aria structure, ensembles, the chorus, dance and pantomime, the orchestra, the prelude and overture. These elements have been examined in a nonhistorical way, in an attempt to show that even though external details of musical and dramatic style have changed, many of the basic concepts and structures of opera have carried through various periods of music history.

These elements exist in opera only to contribute to the total work. Concentration on any of them, at the expense of others, can lead only to misunderstanding of the nature of opera. This is what has happened in this country, unfortunately: fascination with the personalities and techniques of individual singers, and with the music that enables them to display these personalities and techniques to best advantage, has led to an attitude toward opera which ignores almost everything else.

This last chapter will take a successful opera, analyze it closely to show how the previously discussed components are integrated into a work of art, and point out how this art is unique, drawing on both music and drama but achieving effects possible to neither in their pure form. Verdi's *Otello* has been chosen partly for its excellence and partly because it is a complex work drawing on almost all of the elements previously discussed. Since it would be impractical to discuss the entire opera, only one act, the second, will be examined.

A few general comments about this opera, first. *Otello* was Verdi's next to last work, preceding *Falstaff*. The first performance was in

Milan, at the famous La Scala opera, on February 5, 1887; the composer had turned out operas at the rate of about one each year in his younger days, but had not written one for sixteen years, since *Aida* in 1871. It had been assumed by many that *Aida* was his last work, and that Verdi was simply too old to write another opera, but as the composer approached his seventieth birthday there were indications that his creative life was far from over. Two of his earlier operas were performed in radically revised versions—*Simon Boccanegra*, first performed in 1857, was presented in a new version in 1881, and *Don Carlo* of 1867 was revised in 1884—and there was much talk that the old man was working on a new opera based on the Shakespearean drama *Othello*. He commissioned Boito, himself a successful opera composer, to do the libretto, and first planned to call the work *Iago*, after the character who interested him most.

Verdi had long since been recognized as one of the great creative artists of the century, and opera being such a popular form of art-entertainment in Italy, he was very much a national hero. There was an enormous amount of interest, curiosity, and even apprehension as the date of the first performance of the new opera approached. On the one hand, there was excitement at the prospect of a new work from the pen of the creator of *La Traviata, Aida, Rigoletto, Il Trovatore*, and many other deservedly popular operas, but on the other there was apprehension that Verdi was too old to compose successfully any more, and that the occasion would prove to be a tragedy of a sort not planned.

The cast included the great dramatic baritone Victor Maurel as Iago; Francesco Tamagno, said to have the largest tenor voice ever heard in Italy, as Otello; and the soprano Romilda Pantaleoni, a favorite of the conductor, Franco Faccio, as Desdemona. Singers, managers, impresarios, other composers, and the generally curious came from all over Europe. Tickets were sold out days before the premier, and streets leading to the theater were jammed with people who could not get in but wanted to be part of the general excitement. The audience's verdict was apparent before the first act was over: there were repeated applause and calls for the composer even before the act ended, and the applause and shouting were deafening when he took a bow at the end of the act. A cheering throng awaited him outside the theater, and when he finally made his way to his carriage, members of the crowd unharnessed the horses and pulled the triumphant composer through the streets to his destination. Enthusiasm for the work has remained high since; it has been one of his most highly praised operas, by critics and historians, and it has remained in the repertory of most of the major opera houses to the present day.

Verdi had become familiar with the late works of Richard Wagner, which at that time were whipping audiences in the northern part of Europe into frenzied adulation of the great German genius and his "Music of the Future." Many people, then and since, believed that Wagner had created an entirely new art form and had found a new solution to the problem of writing a musical-dramatic work. Observing traces of these same techniques in the later works of Verdi, they have assumed that there was a direct influence. But even though it is entirely possible that familiarity with Wagner's techniques brought about some alterations in detail, it is a mistake to think that there is a sharp stylistic break between *Otello* and Verdi's earlier works. Everything that happens in *Otello* can be traced back to the operas of his middle and even early periods. Verdi and Wagner were both men of the nineteenth century. Their works are more similar, in more ways, than either would have liked to admit, but this similarity stems not so much from any direct influence of one on the other as from the respect and knowledge both had for great operatic works of the past and present, and the sensitivity both had for the most important contemporary currents in music, literature, politics, and society in general.

Critics have pointed out that Verdi abandoned the concept of "number opera" for music drama in *Otello*. It is true that there is no listing of separate sections prefacing the score, no numbering of the various parts of an act, and that there are few pronounced breaks in the music itself to make it clear that one section has ended and another is to begin. But as surely as in his very first opera, each act is built of a succession of contrasting "numbers." Verdi has not labelled them, and there is often connecting music, but there is no mistaking the structure:

OTELLO, ACT II

1. Orchestral prelude		
2. Recitative—Arioso	*"Non ti crucciar"*	Iago, Cassio
3. Recitative—Aria	*"Credo in un Dio crudel"*	Iago
4. Recitative—Pantomime	*"Eccola . . . Cassio . . . a te"*	Iago
5. Recitative—Arioso	*"Cio m'accora"*	Iago, Otello
6. Chorus—Pantomime	*"Dove guardi splendono"*	chorus
7. Recitative—Arioso	*"D'un uom che geme"*	Otello, Desdemona
8. Quartet	*"Forse perche"*	Otello, Desdemona, Iago, Emilia

9. Duet		Iago, Otello
a. Recitative	*"Desdemona rea!"*	both
b. Recitative—Arioso	*"Tu? Indietro!"*	Otello
c. Recitative	*"Pace, Signor"*	both
d. Song	*"Era la notte"*	Iago
e. Recitative—Aria	*"Oh! Monstruosa colpa"*	both

Boito's libretto has often been called the best one written in Italian in the entire nineteenth century. It was written by a man who was a skilled poet, a music critic, and a composer himself, a man who understood perfectly the peculiar and unique requirements of a libretto and how a composer's mind would work when he set it to music. Boito followed Shakespeare's drama faithfully, up to a point; when he made alterations, they were generally those necessary to transform it from a spoken drama into an operatic libretto. Some of Shakespeare's scenes have been eliminated altogether, on occasion several have been condensed to a single operatic scene, and there is much text in the opera not found in the original at all. Despite all this, the spirit and essential structure of the drama have been retained. Enthusiasts have even suggested that Boito's version, with its condensations and additions, is a superior drama to the original—a claim which few English-speaking audiences can take seriously.

Before discussing the second act in detail, a quick summary of the events of the first act might be useful. Otello, a Moor in the service of Venice, returns with his fleet after a victory over the Turks, and is hailed by the people of Cyprus. Otello has made Cassio his lieutenant; Iago, who had wanted the post, is determined to get revenge for this slight. During a victory celebration, Iago presses drink on Cassio and provokes an argument between him and Roderigo, knowing that both had been attracted to Otello's wife Desdemona before she married the Moor. Montano, former governor of Cyprus, intervenes in the dispute and is attacked and wounded by the drunken Cassio. Otello appears, restores order, and dismisses Cassio from his service. The act ends with a love duet between Otello and Desdemona.

1. Orchestral Prelude. The preliminary orchestral music before the curtain rises on the second act has the function of a prelude, too brief to stand by itself as an independent piece. Its function is to set the mood of the opening scene and to state some of the musical material which will be heard in this act. Iago dominates this part of the opera, and the prelude is built appropriately on two themes associated with him. We first hear a violent figure in the lower strings which will be used to characterize him in his most evil moods:

This changes almost immediately into a bland, simply harmonized melody, almost trite in nature, which will be used to suggest the sly, scheming side of his personality.

After a mere 16 measures of treatment of these two ideas, the curtain rises on a room on the first floor of the palace, with a glass door at the rear through which a garden with a terrace can be seen.

    2. *Recitative—Arioso.* Iago and Cassio are talking when the curtain goes up. Since the audience does not know why the two are there, or what has happened, if anything, since the first act ended, the librettist's main job is to write an information-giving section and the composer's is to set this to music which will in no way hinder the listeners' comprehension of it. The librettist tells us what we need to know: Iago is promising Cassio that if he does as he is told, he may regain his position and the admiration of Bianca; the plan is for Cassio to ask Desdemona, "the leader of our leader," to intercede with Otello in his behalf; Iago assures him that Desdemona's nature is such that she will certainly help him, and that he should wait for her on the terrace, where she always comes at this time of day with Iago's wife, Emilia. Cassio agrees to all this and goes out to the terrace, still visible to the audience. Iago watches him until he is out of earshot, then reverts to his true self and snarls, "*Vanne; la tua meta gia vedo . . . .*" The groundwork is thus laid for the plot

which is to ensnare Otello and bring about the final tragedy—set, as is necessary in opera, in recitative.

The librettist offers this information in simple, straightforward language. This is no time for flowery rhetoric or obscure imagery. One of the current English translations, incidentally, is a splendid example of just what the librettist took pains to avoid: "Nay, do not fret. Trust but in me, I promise Thou'lt bask once more in the bright-beaming glances of Mistress Bianca, as dapper a lieutenant, as e'er thou wert, with gilded hilt and baldric. . . ."

In opera of an earlier period, such a scene would have been set by the composer as simple secco recitative. The singers would have delivered their lines to inexpressive, stereotyped recitative formulas, to the neutral accompaniment of a harpsichord and some low stringed instrument. But a composer of the late nineteenth century was usually anxious to use any and all available musical resources to intensify the expression of the text—at all times, even in recitative. Verdi sets the first few lines in old-style recitative, with no help from the orchestra.

But almost immediately, as Iago unfolds his plan to Cassio with a great show of innocence, more melodic and expressive fragments are heard, first in the orchestra,

and then in the voice.

Tu dèi sa - per   che Des-de-mo-na

Recitative shades over into arioso, with melodic material appropriate to the dramatic situation. Iago is pretending to be Cassio's friend, offering to help him, reassuring him that everything will turn out well in the end. The melodic line is bland, routine, trivial, as are the accompanying harmonies. Iago is hiding his true intentions behind his insincere protestations of friendship for Cassio; so Verdi hides Iago's true musical self, already revealed in the first act, behind commonplace melodic and harmonic ideas. It is only when Cassio leaves that Iago shows his real mood. We hear this first in the orchestra, before he says a word: the simple, repetitious, trite motive which has run innocuously through the scene to this point suddenly becomes savage, nasty, ferocious, through an abrupt change of key, dynamics, and orchestration.

IAGO

Van-ne;

The orchestra here is given the function of informing us of a change of mood, of telling us something about the intentions of a character before he states them. The singer's posture, gestures, and even facial expression should intensify this mood, but it comes first and most strongly from the orchestra. Before Iago says a word, the orchestra tells us, in effect, "What has gone before has been false. Now that Cassio has gone, I can give vent to my true feelings, which are hate and scorn for him." This is one of the things which can happen in opera, and in no other art form.

Though Verdi uses more elaborate musical means in this section than would be found in recitative in an older opera, he is continually on guard to see that his music does not obscure the text. The vocal line stays in a medium register, the text is set syllabically, and the orchestra is used sparingly and lightly. Given performers who sing Italian well, an audience which understands it, and a conductor who properly interprets his role, there is nothing to prevent comprehension of every word of the text of this section—just as the librettist intended.

3. Recitative and Aria: Iago.   To this point, the scene has been built on scene 3 of Act II of Shakespeare's play. But with Iago left alone on the stage, suggesting that an aria is in order, Shakespeare is temporarily forgotten. Since he did not write text suitable for an aria, Boito strikes out on his own.

Iago comes forward, addresses the audience, and sings a recitative and aria beginning "I believe in a merciless God, who made me in his own image. . . ." If the text of this aria were to be inserted in a stage production of the Shakespearean play, it would strike the audience as being unnecessary—and markedly inferior to the rest of the play, in language and concept. But Boito has wisely decided that some music is in order at this time, and his text makes it possible for Verdi to write this music.

The opening recitative is dramatic, accompanied by sinister trills and rough outbursts from the orchestra. But the text is set syllabically, the range of the voice is medium to medium-high, and the orchestra is treated mostly in antiphonal fashion to the voice. Here too, a singer with a large and well-projected voice has no difficulty in making it clear to the audience that Iago is offering his philosophy of life, and having them follow most of this philosophy.

The aria section ("*Credo con fermo cuor* . . .") begins with heavier orchestration, and the singer is now asked to sing with and even against the orchestra. But this accompaniment usually takes the form of simple repeated chords, tremolos, and other figural patterns which give rhythmic and harmonic support to the voice without competing with it for melodic interest. The triplet motive which shadows Iago through most of the opera continues to be heard, and is an important unifying device for this somewhat rambling scene.

Verdi has fashioned both a musical and a dramatic climax for the aria. The voice progresses in syllabic but legato fashion through the text, offering the opinion that life is essentially evil. The orchestration thickens, the range climbs higher, and some of the text can easily be lost. But no matter—interest now is centered on the sound of the singer's voice, and a climax is reached, with the high note that many in the audience have paid to hear, on the line "And I believe that man's life is the sport of evil chance, from the beginning in the cradle . . . ."

But the most telling part of the text is yet to come: "After all this folly comes death. And then? And then? Death is the end. . . ." For some people in the nineteenth century, this was blasphemous, and for Verdi it epitomized the wickedness of this character. Even

though these words occur in the middle of an aria, they are set in simple declamatory style. The orchestra tapers down to a few solemn chords in the lowest instruments, the voice recites these words simply, and the final line is literally whispered at the virtually unprecedented (for Verdi) dynamic level of *ppppp*.

A basic technique of operatic composition has always been alternation of musical and dramatic interest, and Verdi's unerring instinct leads him here, as in so many other places in his works, to highly effective and flexible treatment of his text.

A return to faster, louder music, a final high note for Iago, a few more bars of thundering around in the orchestra, and the aria is over. In the following scene we are back with Shakespeare.

4. *Recitative—Pantomime.* The librettist conceived this brief scene visually, plotting what would be seen as he wrote the text. The words give a running commentary on what is being acted out in pantomime and gesture. Desdemona and Emilia enter the garden at the back of the stage, visible to the audience through the glass doors. The wheels are beginning to turn in Iago's plot, and quick, short figures in the orchestra suggest his nervous concern with what is happening.

The other characters cannot hear Iago as he, in recitative, directs their moves. He is like a sort of puppeteer, manipulating the other people on stage. They do as he suggests not because they hear him, but because he has prepared the situation so carefully. First he mutters that the time has come for Cassio, who has been waiting in the garden, to approach Desdemona. Through the glass doors we see him go up to her, bow, and begin a conversation. Now all that is needed is for Otello to appear, and Iago's melodic line becomes almost arioso as he calls upon Satan to help him at this critical moment,

a - iu - ta,a-iu-ta sà-ta-na il mio ci-men-to!

and as he notes that Desdemona and Cassio are engaging in more intimate conversation. Iago's plea is answered: he sees Otello approaching, and scurries to take up a position leaning against a column watching the two in the garden, pretending not to have seen Otello.

This tiny scene would have been set in secco recitative by an earlier composer. Verdi and Boito make more of it by blending recitative with pantomime, by shading recitative into arioso where appropriate, and by making subtle but expressive use of his orchestra. It is a small but strong link in the chain of scenes making up this act; one of the best features of opera of this period is that librettists and composers were willing to lavish care on scenes which would have been tossed off in routine fashion in earlier periods.

5. Recitative—Arioso: Iago, Otello. Textually, this is again an action scene. After the interlude of Iago's soliloquy, during which the plot came to a temporary halt, it is again moved forward, significantly: Iago, through subtle insinuations, plants a seed of doubt and jealousy in Otello's mind and sees it flower immediately. Once again, it is a scene which could have been set in simple recitative, but this technique was of little interest to Verdi.

The first lines are delivered simply enough, though even here the composer cannot resist putting some semblance of a melodic line in

Nul-la . . . voi qui? u-na va-na vo-ce m'u-scì dal lab-bro . . .

the orchestra, rather than having it strum a few uneventful chords. But almost immediately, Iago's insinuating questions take on an arioso quality.

This is lightly accompanied and syllabic, true enough, but it is far removed from a recitative scene in a Metastasian, or even Mozartian, opera. When Iago echoes Otello's words:

OTELLO: Do you not believe him to be honest?
IAGO: . . . honest?
OTELLO: What do you hide in your heart?
IAGO: What do I hide in my heart, signore?
OTELLO: "What do I hide in my heart, signore?"
            By heavens, you are the echo of my words![1]

Verdi does something possible only in opera, echoing the music as well.

Iago's plan works admirably; Otello is goaded into an outburst of exasperation, and Verdi matches his mood with music of more extended range, louder dynamic level, and fuller use of the orchestra.

[1] Translation by Francis Hueffer.

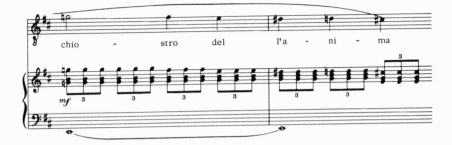

chio - stro del l'a - ni - ma

It is entirely possible that the audience will not understand all of the text here, but with his unerring instinct backed by many decades of experience in writing operas, Verdi uses this kind of setting for lines of text which are not essential to comprehension of what is happening. From what has been said before, from Otello's posture and gestures, from the sound of the music, we understand perfectly well that he is angry at Iago for his insinuations, but is also agitated over the possibility that there might be some basis for them. But when more critical lines of text come along, such as Iago's first use of the word "jealousy," the composer returns to a simple recitative-like style to insure that this will be heard.

Moderato
IAGO

Te - me - te, si - gnor la ge - lo - si - a!

The motive to which Iago sings of the "green-eyed monster" will recur in Act III as Otello's jealousy is fanned.

Otello's last outburst, in which he proclaims that he will not question his wife's virtue unless some evidence is brought before him, is set as dramatic accompanied recitative.

6. *Chorus—Pantomime.* Now Boito and Verdi make another of the shifts away from narration and advancement of the plot so characteristic of opera. There was no chorus in Shakespeare's

play, of course, and whenever one is used in the opera it signals an addition to the original drama. The opening chorus of the first act was narrative, describing the approach of Otello's ship, the storm at sea, the near destruction of the vessel, and its eventual safe entrance into port. But here the chorus is used in another way, as diversion.

Through the glass doors at the back we see Desdemona enter the garden again, this time surrounded by women, children, and sailors, who circle her and offer her flowers and gifts. The children scatter lilies around her, some men present necklaces of coral and pearls, and at the end of the scene Desdemona kisses some of the children and gives the sailors a purse of coins. The group sings folk-like melodies, accompanied by onstage musicians playing bagpipes, small harps, and mandolins.

The scene has no function in the development of the plot. It might be argued that it helps with the characterization of Desdemona by demonstrating that she is kind, generous, and well-loved. But this is characterization of the broadest, most naive sort, which Shakespeare would never have resorted to, and it is unnecessary even in this opera, since Boito and Verdi have drawn a clear picture of her personality elsewhere.

This second act is concentrated and intense, building from the beginning in one simple direction: the arousing of Otello's jealousy by Iago. The chorus, coming almost exactly in the middle of the act, gives momentary relief and sets Otello's mounting jealousy in even sharper relief when it flares up again in the next scene. It is used purely and simply as diversion, as momentary relief from the main drama.

Instead of bringing the previous recitative-arioso section to a complete halt and starting in again with the chorus, Verdi overlaps the two. The first 8 measures of the chorus are heard from off stage, as Iago is telling Otello to observe Desdemona closely for signs of deceit, and as the chorus comes into sight at the back of the stage, following Desdemona, Iago whispers "Here she is . . . be on the lookout. . . ."

The three principals—Otello and Iago at the front of the stage, Desdemona at the back—join the chorus briefly at the very end of the scene. The texts they sing are of no consequence, and cannot be heard in any event. Verdi is merely falling back on the practice popular in nineteenth-century Italian opera of allowing everyone on stage to join in at the end of a concerted piece.

       7. Recitative—Arioso. The chorus leaves, to a brief orchestral postlude, Desdemona comes through the glass doors to join Otello, and we are back to Shakespeare. The ensuing dialogue between the two is another conversational, narrative section in the libretto, with several ideas presented in rapid sequence and abrupt changes in mood. But again Verdi is not content to leave his music at the level of stereotyped recitative-like patterns supported by occasional noncommital chords, but rather draws on any compositional devices that will serve to underline and intensify what is being said.

Desdemona asks Otello to restore Cassio to his service, and Otello is displeased to discover what appears to be confirmation of suspicions aroused by Iago's insinuations. He roughly refuses to consider the matter. This first bit of dialogue is accompanied by an arioso-like melody in the strings, Desdemona's music, its simplicity and sweetness intended to reflect her personality. She sings her lines to this melody, in unison with the orchestra.

But when Otello sings, it is not to the same melody (which continues, however, in the orchestra) but to blunt declamatory phrases which emphasize his refusal to go along with her, to enter into her mood, to agree to her wishes.

Desdemona, abandoning her pleas for Cassio, questions her husband about his ill humor. The two are still in contrasting moods,

Desdemona gently concerned lest her husband be ill, Otello brusque and angry as suspicion and jealousy build up inside him. Verdi makes this contrast vivid by having Otello sing abrupt, short phrases punctuated by sharp, forceful chords in the orchestra, while Desdemona answers with a simple, sweet, legato line.

It is in sections such as this, fluctuating between recitative and arioso, with much of Shakespeare's text retained, that the sharpest strokes of characterization are drawn. Perhaps nowhere in the opera is Desdemona's nature more exquisitely sketched than in Verdi's setting of her lines after Otello's angry outburst, "If, my husband, I have unknowingly committed some sin against you . . . ."

8. *Quartet.* This is a brief but rather complex ensemble-quartet, in which both reflection and action take place simultaneously. Musically, Desdemona dominates much of the time. She is in a static emotional state, pleading with her husband for a kind word to show that he is no longer angry with her; this mood has been prepared in the preceding section of recitative, and her vocal part in this quartet is in effect an aria, developing this single mood and unfolding in a symmetrical musical form. She first sings the principal, 3-measure phrase, in the tonic (B♭ major),

repeats it, then gives out the second melody, which is constructed of 2-measure phrases for contrast and moves to the dominant.

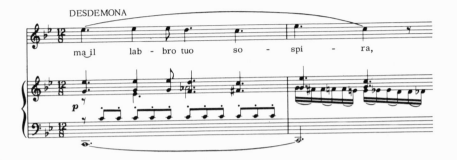

This section ends with a brief extension, built on a cadenza-like figure, and the music returns to B♭, fluctuating between major and minor, with Desdemona singing several phrases representing some sort of variation on the original melody. After a cadence, there is a coda, with the principal melody stated by the orchestra, in the tonic, while she sings a brief countermelody against it. Her part makes perfect musical sense taken by itself, and would make a satisfactory and effective short aria without the other voices.

Otello's mood also carries over from the preceding section: he is despondent over what he believes to be his wife's unfaithfulness, and in a series of short phrases suggests that she no longer loves him because of his lack of social graces, his age, or the color of his skin. The composer has positioned Otello's utterances to fall mostly between Desdemona's phrases, so the two sing mostly in alternation, with some overlap. In the third large division, however (the return to B♭ after Desdemona's brief cadenza), Otello has longer phrases, and often sings with her.

Again, Otello's part makes some sense by itself, though less than Desdemona's. But these two parts would make an excellent duet, with the two in contrasting moods at first, their parts complementing one another musically with their contrasting melodic material, then coming together for the climax.

Meanwhile, the other two characters are engaged in a byplay of their own. Iago, looking ahead to the next step in his plot, asks Emilia to give him Desdemona's handkerchief, which had been a gift from Otello. Emilia, fearful that he is up to no good, refuses to let him have it. He becomes infuriated and finally tears it out of her hand. Their emotional states are in conflict with those of the other two singers, and Verdi gives them quite different music: they sing in short, hurried exclamations, in quick repeated notes which contrast with the more legato lines of Desdemona and Otello.

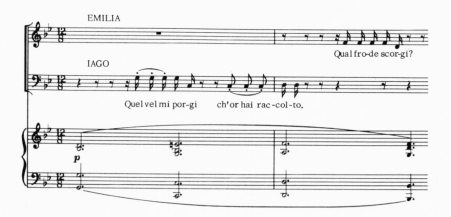

Thus the four characters have four different texts, and at times the audience can grasp none of them. But Desdemona and Otello are singing reflective passages, their texts offering no new information, and the first lines of Iago and Emilia are sung in rapid staccato, parlando style which cuts through the other two voices. In addition, since their quarrel and Iago's eventual capture of the handkerchief is portrayed in pantomime, carefully marked in the score, there is no difficulty in following the dramatic movement of the scene.

The four voices are carefully contrasted in the first two sections, with much of the singing done in consecutive rather than simultaneous fashion, but Verdi brings the third section to a musical climax by having all four sing together, with Iago and Emilia dropping their declamatory delivery, as is shown in the example opposite.

The final section, the coda, is quiet, with the orchestra playing Desdemona's original melody while she addresses a final plea for pardon to Otello, he brusquely asks everyone to leave, and Iago mutters a last threat to Emilia.

9. *Duet—Finale.*   The act does not end with a finale involving a number of the principals and chorus, but rather with a lengthy and complex duet serving the same function of creating a dramatic and musical climax.

The first short section, of recitative, serves as a bridge between

vol - to - - mi - ra co-me fa-vel-la

- ri - gli sem-pre ci guar - di Dio dai pe-ri -

- fran - - - gò e ru - i - nar__ nel fan - gò ve-dò jl mio so - - gno

qui-do, ed o - ra__ su que-sta tra-ma Ia -go la-vo -

the preceding quartet and this final duet. Otello, exhausted from his outbursts, mutters a few phrases of anger and dismay; Iago, standing at the back unseen and unheard by Otello, gloats over the continuing success of his plot and says that as a next step he will hide Desdemona's handkerchief in Cassio's house. This brief scene is a section of musical repose, with the two singers mostly reciting on a single pitch. The orchestra furnishes a sinister undertone, however, with its quiet reiteration of the rising four-note motive which runs through this act, characterizing the evil nature of Iago.

The plan of the duet calls for an impressive musical ending, with both singers involved, and for each of them to have a solo section of secondary importance leading up to it. It is Otello's turn first, and he is given the stage to himself as he sings a dramatic, accompanied recitative and a brief but intense arioso. First, surprised to find Iago still there, Otello brusquely tells him to leave, since he has already caused him enough anguish. Then his mood changes, and he speaks tenderly of the days of happiness with Desdemona before suspicion intruded. His phrases are short and make frequent use of variations on the most common old-fashioned recitative formulas.

But even here Verdi is shaping his music, not letting it wander aimlessly. After a quiet beginning, Otello's melodic line works toward a climax, moving higher and higher until it reaches a peak on a high A♭; under this, the bass works up a sequential pattern which reaches its high point at the same time.

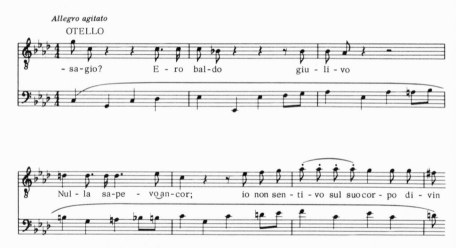

The voice descends gradually, an octave and a fourth, coming to rest on the lowest note of the recitative (E♮) before two final, louder, higher exclamations lead into the arioso. Thus these 20 measures are organized into a simple arch form, beginning at a low level, rising to a peak slightly past the midpoint, and sinking again.

"Farewell" arias have been a staple in Italian opera since the first decades of the history of the form. Shakespeare was not farsighted enough to write a suitable passage for such an occasion into his play; so Boito obliged. Over a strummed accompaniment, with low mutterings of the triplet figure which runs throughout so much of this act, Otello bids farewell to the happy life he has known.

Addio sante memorie,
Addio sublimi incanti del pensier!
Addio schiere fulgenti
Addio vittorie, dardi volanti e volanti corsier!

This goes on for only 22 measures, not enough time for much development of melodic material or complexity of formal design. The music is dramatic and intense, and allows the tenor to display his loud, high notes at the end, but it is an arioso rather than an aria because of its brevity and formal simplicity.

After this momentary pause, the action moves forward again in a scene of narration. The two characters go through several violent changes of mood, and Verdi is concerned here with the forward movement of the play, rather than with any formal musical organization. First Otello charges Iago of making accusations without offering proof, and his anger builds up until he begins to throttle Iago. These lines are delivered in halting, declamatory style against scurrying, nervous, hurried figures in the orchestra.

Otello desists, and Iago again proclaims his innocence and truthfulness (beginning with the line *"Divina grazia difendimi"*), though the orchestra contradicts him by playing fragments of the music associated with his evil scheming. He offers to resign from Otello's service, and makes a pretense of leaving.

In the third section of this recitative, beginning with the line *"Credo leale Desdemona,"* Otello complains of his dilemma: he thinks that his wife is faithful, but again he thinks she is not; he believes Iago, then again he does not. These contradictory statements are mirrored in the music by a rising line in the bass as he suggests that his wife might be honest, then its opposite, a descending line, as he says that she may not be. Iago is now ready to play his trump card:

he almost whispers that if it is proof that Otello wants, he shall have it. He speaks in the simplest recitative style, with light support from the orchestra. Yet if Otello listened to the sounds coming from the pit, he would be forewarned; the low, sinister trills make unmistakable reference back to Iago's evil *"Credo"* aria. He is about to transform his beliefs into actions.

His "proof" is the story of how one night as he was sleeping with Cassio in the barracks, the latter muttered affectionate words to Desdemona in his sleep, warned her to be cautious lest her husband discover what was going on between them, cursed fortune which had given her to Otello, and, still in his sleep, turned to Iago and attempted to kiss and caress him, dreaming that he was Desdemona. This is narration, and Verdi chose to set it in a completely syllabic fashion, within a limited range, with light orchestration, to insure that it all be understood. But it is not recitative: Verdi sets the beginning, and much of the rest of the section as well, in symmetrical phrases with recurring melodic and rhythmic material. It is too melodic and too well-developed musically to be recitative, too limited in its musical means to be aria. It is a brief and incomplete song.

The choice of $\frac{6}{8}$ meter, which gives a gently rocking movement and is often used for lullabies and other music descriptive of sleep, is a subtle touch. Notable also is the dynamic marking *ppppppp* for the second, most telling part of the song. Verdi made it clear on many occasions, in many ways, that certain lines in his operas were to be delivered with more regard for dramatic impact than quality of voice; here, as Iago tells of how Cassio cursed the fortune which had made Desdemona Otello's wife, the composer has no less than three directions in the score to make it clear to the singer that the words are the most important thing here: *"parlando," "cupo,"* and *"sempre sotto voce."*

Verdi has a musical climax planned to end this scene (and act), but one more dramatic point must be made first. In a final recitative section beginning with Otello's line *"Oh! monstruosa colpa!"* Iago offers a final bit of proof. He reports that he has seen the handkerchief, which was Otello's first gift to Desdemona, in Cassio's possession. This prompts a final frenzied outburst from Otello, set as dramatic accompanied recitative and leading to the final section of this lengthy duet.

This last section is organized into the simplest, most symmetrical musical form of the entire act. The dramatic content is negligible: Otello swears vengeance for the wrongs which he is now convinced have been done him, and Iago swears to help him. This is a traditional aria situation, with a static dramatic point reached so that music can take its own course. The principal melody is given out first by the orchestra, against Otello's first line of text,

and the rounded musical form ABACABA develops, with the main melody sung each time by Iago, either alone or with Otello. The phrases are mostly balanced, 4 or 8 measures in length, and at the end the two men sing together in a last musical climax, which is rounded off by a few loud measures from the orchestra, built of chord sequences characteristic of this act.

A summary seems unnecessary. Verdi has drawn on all possible elements of opera in this act, used them in a flexible, subtle, and imaginative way, and has created a work of art in which primary interest is now in the music, now in the drama, sometimes in both— but which is never pure music or drama. It is opera.

INDEX

Louise (Charpentier), 12
Lucia di Lammermoor (Donizetti),
6, 11, 71 f., 115 f.
Lully, Jean-Baptiste:
dance in operas, 176 f.
use of orchestra, 131–133
Lulu (Berg), 174

Macbeth (Verdi), 10, 157, 182
Madame Butterfly (Puccini), 7, 11,
54–56, 150
Magic Flute, The (Mozart), 2, 5, 6,
9, 10, 13, 23, 50 f., 67
male voices, classification of, 8 ff.
Manon (Massenet), 28, 181 f.
Manon Lescaut (Puccini), 9
Marriage of Figaro, The (Mozart),
7, 11, 12, 52 f., 66, 98–100,
171 f.
Masked Ball, A (Verdi), 8, 162, 185
Mathis der Maler (Hindemith),
152, 170
Matrimonio Segreto, Il (Cimarosa),
197–201
Medium, The (Menotti), 8, 11, 15,
26, 190 f.
Mefistofele (Boito), 12
Meistersinger, Die (Wagner), 5, 6,
10, 90, 105, 157
melodrama, 28 ff.
Menotti, Gian Carlo:
overtures, 172
on recitative, 34 f.
recitative-aria structure, 58–61
Metastasio, Pietro, 45 f., 48, 68 f.,
192
mezzo-soprano voice, 7 f.
Midsummer Night's Dream (Britten), 18 f.
Mignon (Thomas), 164 f.
Mond, Der (Orff), 26
Moses und Aron (Schoenberg), 184
Mother of Us All, The (Thomson),
4, 160
Mozart, Wolfgang Amadeus:
as composer of finales, 98 ff.
and music drama, 210
orchestra, 140

Mozart, Wolfgang Amadeus
(cont.):
overtures, 171 f.
stage directions in, 193 f.
music drama, 197 ff., 201 ff., 208,
210 f., 216
musical characterization, 76–78,
85 f.
musical comedy, 24, 43

Neapolitan opera, 134 ff.
Norma (Bellini), 94–98
Noye's Fludde (Britten), 18
number opera, 197 ff., 208, 210 f.,
216, 219 f.

obbligato accompaniment to arias,
136 f.
octet, 68
Oedipus der Tyrann (Orff), 175
Oedipus Rex (Stravinsky), 175
offstage music, 156 ff.
onstage music, 156 ff., 230
opera, contrasted with spoken
drama, 79, 81 f.
opéra-comique, 24, 43
operetta, 24, 43
orchestra, 125 ff., 158
accompanying melodrama, 28
accompanying pantomime,
189 ff.
accompanying singers, 140 ff.
expansion of with Monteverdi,
127–130
used to depict characters, 150
Orfeo (Monteverdi), 32, 127–130,
160, 183, 192
Orfeo ed Euridice (Gluck), 2, 20,
119 f., 186
ornamentation, in singing, 20, 127,
134
Otello (Verdi), 150, 217–239
Ottone (Handel), 138 f.
overture, 159 ff., 175
as call to attention, 159 f.
formalized overture, 167–174
miscellaneous types, 174 f.

Turn of the Screw (Britten), 2, 18, 157

Vanessa (Barber), 11, 90, 157, 185, 187
Verdi, Guiseppe:
    as composer of ensembles, 82 ff.
    contrast with Wagner, 219
Vestale, La (Spontini), 149
vocal range, effect on text, 38 f.
voices:
    classification of, 3 ff.
    and roles, 11 ff.

Wagner, Richard, 219
    scenes in recitative, 62–65
    size of orchestra, 146
    and traditions of opera, 213 f.
    use of *leitmotif*, 151
    use of onstage music, 157 f.
    use of stage directions, 195 f.
Walküre, Die (Wagner), 150, 195 f., 212–214
Werther (Massenet), 12 f., 107 f.
Wilde, Oscar, 201 ff.
William Tell (Rossini), 12, 102, 122–124, 182
Wozzeck (Berg), 15, 39, 162, 185